Oh Really, Riley?

Oh Really, Riley?

The Complete Story of Riley's Trick Shop and the Family Behind It

Jim Riley

ISBN: 1508702470
ISBN 13: 9781508702474

To my wife Judy, my business and life partner.
Thanks for your patience and understanding
as I tapped out these pages day after day.
Mere words will never convey all you mean to me.

To all our loyal customers through the years
without whose support we'd have
to go out and get real jobs.

To Jim and Eleanor Riley
without whom none of this
would be possible.

Jim and Eleanor Riley on their 60th Anniversary

Preface

You are about to embark on a journey of one man's dream and where it took him. He did not see its end. Your humble scribe had the sad task of overseeing its fate.

The story's title comes from the standard response whenever I'd relate any of the happenings I'm about to tell you. If I had a dollar for every time I've heard it, I'd have no need to work, or write this book.

Everything you're about to read is true. Some of the dialogue may not be exact, there was no one taking down every word, but it's true to the people who said it. The story of the later years comes from my daily journal and personal experiences. The early years are based on the countless times I'd heard these stories from my parents. I'd roll my eyes on hearing them over and over, but that's how they stuck with me.

I decided to write this story for several reasons, chiefly to set the record straight on where our stores have been through the years. If we'd been on every corner and block people thought we were on, we'd have had more locations than Starbucks.

Typical was the woman who said, "I remember your store on 69th and Langley" to my Dad. When he answered that we were never at that intersection, she got in his face and told him, "What do *you* know? I was in your store at 69th and Langley and don't you tell me any different." You'll see his response repeated throughout the story. It was one of his favorite sayings.

I wrote this also to hark back to a time when a man could take a dream of being his own boss and turn it into reality without having it crushed by giant, soulless conglomerates.

I wanted everyone to know definitively that we never were associated with Ryan's Trick Shop, Wayne's Trick Shop, Bill's Trick Shop, Chuck's House of Magic, or Izzy Rizzy's House of Tricks. There has been much confusion over the years. We knew them all well and worked with them on occasion but they are gone and now so are we.

It's about a family business where we got to know our customers and they came to know us. Not many businesses could claim that a customer from the 1970s could come into the same store in the same location in the new millennium and see the same face he or she saw back then. Granted, that face had more lines than they remembered and there was a lot less hair on the head above it, but it was the same face nonetheless.

Finally, I wrote it so future generations of Rileys will know the legacy left them by two children of immigrants.

Thanks to Cheryl Bouselli of Paper Magic Group for information regarding the early years of one of our suppliers.

Special thanks to Don and Joyce Wiberg for inviting me into their home and spending a delightful afternoon reminiscing about the days at Riley's before I was born.

If you'd like to see more of our story in pictures, you can go to the Riley's Trick Shop page on Facebook and look through our history album.

Jim Riley

Prologue

I t was always there. Since the day I was born I was a part of it. It was the source of everything I ever had. It kept a roof over my head and food on my table. Even my parents who started it and were involved for more than sixty years, lived the first third of their lives without it. To us it was "the store." To everyone else in the Chicago area and around the world, thanks to the internet, it was known as Riley's Trick Shop.

Founded in 1937 by my parents, Jim and Eleanor Riley, Riley's Trick Shop was the source of fun for generations on the South Side of Chicago. Parents brought their kids and then their grandkids to stock up on joy buzzers, whoopie cushions, fake puke, and other treats. Countless former Chicagoans made it a point to stop by when they were back in town. They brought their grandchildren, too.

Riley's wasn't always a trick shop and this is the story.

In The Beginning

James Joseph Robert Riley was born on Chicago's East Side on September 16, 1908, and grew up in the area near 92nd and Commercial, a gritty neighborhood of steel mills, docks, and taverns. His parents, James Riley and Anna Malloy, arrived from County Mayo, Ireland, sometime in the 1890s. He was the youngest of three children. His brother, Martin, would go on to work at the water filtration plant near Rainbow Beach on Lake Michigan. His sister, Mary, taught in the Chicago Public Schools for 42 years. Jim started working at an early age, selling *The Industrialist*, the organ of the International Workers of the World, also known as the Wobblies. It seems strange that this future entrepreneur would hawk a paper that espoused the overthrow of capitalism but, hey, a buck's a buck.

He didn't talk much about his early years except that he was an altar boy at St. Patrick's Church on Ewing Avenue and graduated from St. Pat's school in 1925. That's what it said on the roadmap-sized diploma we found among his things. We never did find out why he graduated grammar school at the age of seventeen. After a semester at Mt. Carmel High School he was expelled for shooting dice in the hallway. From then on it was work, work, work. His mother once told him he'd never die in bed.

It was around this time that his father died in an accident involving a Chicago Transportation Authority street car. Depending on which relative you ask, he either walked in front of the car where the motorman didn't see him and ran him over or he slipped going out the door and had a fatal head injury. For that, the CTA paid Anna the princely sum of $600. Anna passed away in 1944.

He made friends wherever he went but his life-long pals were from the South Chicago neighborhood. In most cities they're called gangs but in Chicago they're referred to as "social clubs." His was called "The Chevaliers." As adults, they dispersed around the country but always kept in touch. On our summer road trips, we made stops in places like Albuquerque, San Francisco, Seattle, and Ft. Lauderdale to stop by and say hello. Sometimes that hello would result in being put up for three days or more.

Jim Riley, seated at left with The Chevaliers, late 20's.

Jim knocked around a series of jobs in the 20's and early 30's eventually winding up in the grocery business at the Piggly-Wiggly. Their stores had a unique setup: once the customer entered, she had to traverse a serpentine path to the checkout which required her to pass every item on the shelves. This clever piece of marketing probably led to more things in her grocery basket than were on the original list.

These were not the warehouse-sized mega-supermarkets we frequent to-day. Grocery stores occupied one or two storefronts on a busy street. There were no parking lots. If you were lucky enough to own a car, you parked on the street. Most people walked, carrying their purchases in a grocery bag or dragging folding two-wheeled carts behind them for larger orders. A shopping cart never left the store. Jim worked himself up to manager of a National Tea store and that's where he met his future wife.

Eleanor Virginia Borgeson, the only child of Nathaniel (Nate) Borgeson and Ellen Ahlin, was born in Chicago on March 3, 1915. Nate emigrated from Goteborg, Sweden, in 1905. Total cost for the ship to New York and train to Chicago was $48. You can bet it wasn't first class. Eleanor was an avid historian and the original documents were in the papers she left. Nate and Ellen married in 1913.

The family moved to Lockport, Illinois, where Eleanor grew up. Like Jim she was a hard worker who got up at 4 a.m. to walk from her house at Jefferson and Division down the hill to a bakery on State Street to help start the baking for the day. From there she went to school.

The same year that Jim's father died, Eleanor's mother succumbed to food poisoning after eating an apple from a tree that had been sprayed with insecticide. Nate died in 1948 while my mother was carrying me. I never got to meet any of my grandparents.

Eleanor graduated from Lockport High School in 1932 and moved back to Chicago with her father. She eventually went to work in the grocery business. It was at the National Tea where she met Jim.

Being Irish, Jim was always quick with a story but it was hard to tell if he was telling the truth or just making it up for effect. The story of how he and Eleanor got engaged is typical. One evening, so the story goes, he was having dinner with Eleanor and Nate at their place. Nate asked Jim if he wanted another pork chop. At the same time Eleanor asked him if he wanted to marry her. When he said "yes" he got a pork chop and a fiancee.

Jim's sister had purchased a piece of property west of Twin Lakes near Dowagiac, Michigan, in 1929. She originally wanted to build a cottage near the lake but her mother suggested she build on a hill to get the breeze. The summer humidity could be stifling. The cottage had two bedrooms with two beds each in back and a combination living room, dining room, and kitchen in front. It had indoor plumbing but water had to be pumped from a well by hand. The dining/living room had sofas and chairs but the centerpiece was a huge, round wooden table, the kind supported in the center by a heavy pedestal with ornate carved feet. It was the gathering place where many a poker hand was played, story swapped, meal enjoyed, and beer consumed. Mary covered the outside of the cottage with a unique shape of shingle in shamrock green. They named the place WeLikeIt.

Jim, leaning in doorway at the WeLikeIt cottage.

Like it they did. Jim and Eleanor would close the National at 8 p.m. Saturday night and pile whoever could fit in his Oldsmobile to head up there to enjoy a summer Sunday. Some even made the four-hour trip standing on the running boards when the seats were full. It's a good bet that not much sleeping went on but everyone was back at work Monday morning.

Rhodes Avenue

A Store Is Born

Chicago is based, thanks to Daniel Burnham's master plan, on a grid of major streets a mile apart. East and west there are sixteen streets to a mile, north and south, eight. Storefronts and offices are at ground level on the major streets with apartments or more offices above. On side streets there were sometimes stores between the main street and a parallel alley. It was next to the alley on the east side of one of those side streets in the Chatham neighborhood (or St. Dorothy's parish if you were Catholic) between Cottage Grove and South Park, south of 79th Street, that Jim Riley and Eleanor Borgeson opened their store on Sunday, March 21, 1937. The address was 7909 Rhodes. Their first customer was Irene Keller, the wife of Joe Keller who owned Keller's Tap around the corner on 79th Street.

By today's standards it wasn't much of a store. It seemed big to me when I was a kid but I was only eight when we left. By looking at some old pictures and making some very uneducated guesses I estimate it couldn't have been more than 20 feet wide and 30 to 40 feet deep. The front was two display windows flush with the sidewalk. Two more windows angled toward a door in the middle. Inside the door to the right were glass and wood showcases. That was the counter where business was transacted. Behind them against the wall were shelves. The lower half was filled with drawers originally used as storage for 5x8 index cards. The upper half was where larger items were kept. To the left of the door were taller glass showcases that angled back from the floor. They may have come from a bakery or candy store. None of it was new. All the cases were originally filled with stationery, greeting cards, board games, and notions. Notions are defined as "small, useful items or sundries." Since Eleanor was a seamstress, there were lots of sewing items like packages of needles, thread and thimbles. Basically, it was a general store. They even took in laundry and shipped packages.

In a throwback to his gambling days that got him kicked out of high school, Jim somehow got the phone number Stewart 7411, as in "seven for eleven." He kept that number until 1965. The phone company inserted a 3 before the 7 when phone numbers went from six to seven digits.

Three weeks after the store opened, Jim and Eleanor were married on Sunday, April 11, 1937, at Our Lady of Peace Church at 79th and Jeffrey. It wasn't much of a wedding. Since Eleanor wasn't Catholic they couldn't be married in the sanctuary. Instead they had a small ceremony in the rectory with Jim's cousin Dan Malloy and his sister Mary as best man and maid of honor. A small reception netted them a whopping $15.00 in gifts. And so they embarked on a journey that lasted almost 65 years.

The small back room of the store became their home after they were married. There was no living together ahead of time in those days. Their view, through iron security bars, was the single-car garages allotted to each tenant, and the underside of the wooden staircase leading to the back porch of the second floor apartments. In later years Jim would proudly say that he never parked a car in a garage. His garage was for storing merchandise or "stock" as he called it.

There was no bathtub or shower. They had to bathe in a metal tub filled with water dragged by the bucketful from the bathroom sink. For their bedroom Jim brought home a bed, dresser, and vanity he found in the alley. We still have them. Their first purchase was a small Frigidaire refrigerator for $99.00. In later years it became Jim's beer refrigerator. It was still in use when they had their 50th anniversary party.

How's Tricks?

Riley's didn't start off as a trick shop but it wasn't long before its destiny was set. Jim had somehow acquired a counter-top popcorn machine with a glass front where you could watch the popcorn pop. People would stop by to pick up a bag or box before heading to the Rhodes Theater across 79th Street between Rhodes and St. Lawrence because Riley's price was lower than the theater's. When the theater manager found out why his popcorn sales were so low he came into Riley's and offered Jim $75 for the wagon. Jim took that windfall and invested it in a line of tricks, jokes, and magic from the S.S. Adams Company of Neptune, New Jersey. And so a kernel of popcorn expanded into Riley's Trick Shop.

The Rhodes Theater is long gone. Riley's carried the Adams line to the end but the one hundred year old company was recently purchased by Magic Makers who moved it from its long-time home in Neptune, New Jersey, to their headquarters in Sioux Falls, South Dakota.

When that first box of tricks from Adams arrived, Jim was like a kid on Christmas morning. He opened every item and played with it until he knew what it did and how it worked. He was especially intrigued by the magic tricks. The stationery and other items of the original stock were pushed into smaller spaces and replaced by items from Adams and other novelty companies. It wasn't long before everyone on the South Side knew that Riley's Trick Shop was *the* place for jokes and magic.

The Early Years

Even though the Depression had eased somewhat, the country didn't fully recover until the wartime economy brought about by World War II. The late thirties were not the best time to start a business but the store did well. The ledger from 1937 showed that they took in a whopping $1800 for the month of October, their first Halloween. In later Halloweens we'd do that much in an hour. The ledger also showed their monthly bills: telephone $2.62, electricity $3.28, rent $45.00.

In front of the store there was a parkway between the sidewalk and Rhodes Avenue. Eleanor's father, Nate, built a couple of benches and set them facing each other in the parkway. Nate worked at the store, too. Many a slow hour was spent on those benches in warmer weather. It wouldn't surprise anyone if more than one beer was consumed during those hours, too. They could keep an eye on the entrance to the store and listen for the phone while swapping stories and visiting with neighbors passing by.

There was no air conditioning so a screen door provided what breeze there might be to cool the store. Screen doors in those days were basically a wood frame of one by threes with mesh attached to it. A long spring was the closer and it would slam the door multiple times if you didn't hold it on its return. The sound was a resounding WHAP followed by several quieter and more closely-spaced whaps. Every kid must have heard at least a thousand times growing up, "Don't slam the (WHAP) door."

Always one to take advantage of an opportunity to play a joke, Jim put a second handle on the other side of the screen door. The unwary customer had a 50-50 chance of getting the right one. If he grabbed the wrong one he'd look like a fool when the door didn't open.

Another door joke was a fake doorbell. It looked just like any other doorbell that was common in those days: round with a button in the middle. Just about every home had one so no one would question one on Riley's door frame. Jim's button had one big difference--there was a pin in the middle. When the button was pushed, the visitor got his finger pricked and it usually drew blood. Imagine trying to get away with that these days.

Another of his favorites was the Auto Bomb, also known as the Auto Fooler, a cardboard cylinder with a wire running through it. One end of the wire is attached to a spark plug and the other to any metal ground on the car. When the wired plug fires, the wire instantly heats up and ignites the charge inside. It whistles like one of those World War II bombs coming down, then smoke pours out from under the hood. In those days it exploded, too. Fireworks were legal in Illinois back then.

Jim had a setup with Nick Manola who owned the barber shop next door. One of them would distract a customer while the other put one of these bombs on his car. Cars back then had no hood locks and the motors were simple affairs where everything was out in the open. An auto bomb could be installed in under 30 seconds, even on a bad day. When the customer started his car and the bomb went off, Jim and Nick ran out of their stores and doused the victim's car with buckets of water they kept near their front doors.

Another running gag he had with Nick was to pretend he was waiting for a haircut and get into an argument with him while the victim was being shaved. As the argument got more heated, Nick would wave his just-stropped straight razor around the victim's face in mock anger. At the climax Jim would get up and push Nick as he dragged the razor across the victim's throat. Of course, he would have secretly secured the blade in the razor's handle. The victim would jump out the chair screaming as Nick and Jim rolled howling on the floor. This continued until the inevitable happened. Nick didn't get the razor fully-secured in time and sliced the victim's ear. Today this would have resulted in a lawsuit, but the victim became a good customer of both businesses--once the bleeding stopped.

The late thirties were a heady time for Jim and Eleanor. The business was growing and they were having a great time. There were the weekend trips to the WeLikeIt cottage and long vacations on the road.

In 1938 they packed up their '36 Olds and headed west. Road trips in those days were not the luxurious affairs they are today. Cars had no air conditioning and were notoriously unreliable. Radios were an expensive option. Out west there weren't many stations to listen to anyway. Interstate highways had yet to be thought of and most roads were two-lane highways that passed through every little town on the way. In other words, a road trip was an experience.

It was probably because car travel was such an adventure that Jim and Eleanor made friends everywhere they went. If an upcoming section of highway was especially difficult or desolate, caravans would sometimes form at the "last chance" service station. If a car broke down or had a flat tire on the way, there would be someone to help. Over a meal or drink at a diner at the other end they would exchange addresses and promise to write. Eleanor kept that promise and spent her Sunday mornings writing to these folks for the rest of her life.

Motels were few and far between, too. One night they had to share a room in some town in the middle of nowhere. It was getting dark and the road ahead was treacherous even in the daytime. Since it was the last room for miles in any direction they decided to share it with another couple, a cab driver and his wife, who were also looking at a night sleeping in their car. For a little privacy they found a way to hang a sheet between the two beds. There was no TV. Small town radio stations usually shut down after dark so the only entertainment was talking. The cabbie, who was used to chatting up his fares, talked all night. Every time he wanted to make a point he'd poke his head around the sheet. It's a good bet that nobody got much sleep that night. If they exchanged addresses in the morning it's a better bet that couple didn't make Eleanor's short list for writing back.

The War Years

December 7, 1941, brought lots of changes to the country. Many of Jim's friends found themselves in the armed forces after the Japanese attack on Pearl Harbor. Dan Malloy, his best man, joined the Marines and saw action in the Pacific. One of the Chevaliers, Bill Hannon, made the local news for surviving a direct hit by a coconut. It seems the enemy fruit detached itself from a palm tree and scored a direct on his unprotected head as he relaxed under the tree. It was newsworthy because he was one of the few US servicemen to survive such an attack. For Jim there were no such adventures. He was thirty-three and the doctor thought he had a heart problem.

He contributed to the war effort in his own way. Every block had a captain in the service of the Office of Civil Defense. Jim was the block captain for the east and west sides of Rhodes from 79th to 80th. His duty was to make sure every light was turned off during air raid drills. He even got his picture in the Tribune when he retrieved a "bomb" from one of those drills. The "bombs" consisted of rolled-up strips of newspaper with crepe paper streamers dropped from airplanes. Eleanor put that "bomb" in her scrapbook. I still have it.

The steel mills were working three shifts to keep up with production for the war effort but there weren't enough men left Stateside to keep up. After working a full day at the store, Jim would close each evening and head to the US Steel plant on Lake Michigan at the east end of 79th Street to work the graveyard shift. Sleep came in shifts, too, a few hours in the evening and again in the morning. That almost caught up to him one night. He must have been exhausted to fall asleep amid the noise and heat of the mill, but sleep he did. What woke him up he never knew, but it was just in time to get out of the way of crane carrying a load of molten steel. From that night on, Eleanor made sure he napped during the day while she watched the store.

Another change brought about by the war was rationing. Access to just about everything was restricted, if it was available at all. Everyone was affected by rationing but Riley's was affected most by the shortage of rubber because it was used in the manufacture of Halloween masks. During October Jim would stop by Don Post Studios on the South Side after his shift at the mill to pick up what masks he could. There were always customers waiting when he got home.

Don Post was the originator of the Halloween mask. He started out making masks of Hitler, Mussolini, and Stalin in 1939. He was later discovered by film makers, moved to Hollywood, and made masks for Star Wars and Planet of the Apes, among other movies. His masks are coveted by collectors around the world. His son, Don, runs the business today.

Masters of Magic

Even as the war took its toll on the country, the store thrived. It became a gathering place for local amateur conjurers in addition to any professional magicians who might be performing in town. State Street in the Loop was lined with theaters from the old Vaudeville days and the performers would visit the local magic shops looking to meet other magicians or find anything new they could add to their acts. On these visits they'd autograph black and white 8x10 photos of themselves. The wall behind Riley's magic counter became lined with glossies of all the greats: Blackstone, Dante, Cardini, Thurston, Don Alan, and many others.

In 1944 a group of Jim's magic customers decided to form a club. The Magic Masters of Chicago was organized September 27, 1944, in the store by John Benson, John Buck, Bill Dunbaugh, Oscar Johnston, John McCarthy, Bob Nelson, William Reda, Jim Riley, and Stanley Toy. The first meeting was held in December 1944 with Bill Dunbaugh as president in 1945. Jim Riley took over as president the next year and was the club's treasurer for many years.

The early meetings were held in the store but Eleanor complained about the smoke and noise going on into the wee hours of the morning. It wasn't more than a fifty-foot walk from the back door of Riley's to the back door of Keller's Tap so there were probably more than a few beers consumed, too. Eleanor was not too happy about all the empty beer bottles that she had to clean up before the store opened. Before long, the meetings took place in the back of Manola's barber shop next door. That made Eleanor happy. The guys were happy too because the move cut the walk to Keller's by a good twenty feet.

Magic Masters has thrived over the years. Their annual past presidents banquet regularly draws a crowd of at least 500. It's been held at various times of the year and different places on the South Side of Chicago. Since 1973 it's been held at the Lexington House in Hickory Hills, Illinois, on the first or second Friday after Easter. For $30 you get an excellent family-style dinner and a magic show on their stage. Sometimes the entire show is a national traveling magic act. Other times it's a combination of professionals, amateurs, and kids. Throw in a juggler or comedian and you have an evening of good, old-fashioned fun.

Magic Masters meet at Riley's, 1945. Eleanor Riley, Nate Borgeson, Jim Riley at right of counter, left to right.

One More Boomer

As wars do, the "big one" finally came to an end and the troops came home. That led to the post-war baby boom of the late forties and early fifties and the 7900 block of Rhodes saw its fair share. Thinking it was time to start a family, Jim and Eleanor left the back room of the store and moved to an apartment at 7948 Rhodes, a yellow brick U-shaped building on the west side of the street. Theirs was the first entrance on the left, up to the first floor, the door on the right. It was a one-bedroom unit with a living room (or front room, pronounced frunchroom in Chicago) from which a narrow hallway led to a small dining room and a smaller kitchen. The five hundred feet from 7948 to 7909 Rhodes was the farthest Jim Riley would ever have to travel to his beloved store.

Try as they might, it just wasn't in the cards. They suffered through several miscarriages and stillbirths, wondering what they were doing wrong and if they'd ever have a child. Eleanor did everything she could. She even took DES, a drug that was supposed to help high-risk pregnancies come to term. Daughters of those pregnancies had a high percentage of cancer as they reached their adult years. She also played classical music to calm herself and the baby. They had a huge wooden console with cabinets on each side that held thick 78-rpm records. In the middle was a grill with fancy acoustical padding behind it. The bottom half of the grill was a big speaker and the top half was a fold-out shelf which revealed a radio and turntable on top. Eleanor sat there night after night playing Brahms, Beethoven, Mozart, and others in the hope that the baby would be soothed and survive.

Finally, on October 13, 1948, at 3:13 a.m. in the maternity ward of St. George's Hospital in Englewood, I, James Patrick Riley, came into the world at a healthy 6 pounds, 6 ounces. Eleanor and Jim Riley became Mom and Dad Riley.

As Dad paced the halls he ran into Ed O'Toole who owned the candy store/delicatessen two doors north of Riley's, next to Manola's. Each asked the other what he was doing there. Ed explained that his wife, Elinor, had given birth to a girl. Bonnie O'Toole and I became great friends even though she teased me that she was a whole day older. It was actually four hours. We even had combined birthday parties. When the neighborhood changed, the O'Tooles moved to Seattle but they were high on Mom's correspondence list and they kept in touch until Ed and Elinor died. Bonnie and I went our separate ways but she has stopped in to the store a time or two when in town.

All The News That Fits

In May of 1949 Riley's introduced a service that would be an instant hit and an enduring classic. Dad bought a Vandercook Model 1 proof press, a 17 x 32-inch two hundred-pound monster of steel and wood. To that he added a 9A font of 108-point Helvetica Narrow wooden type and went into the fake newspaper headline business. The number of individual letters of type in a font was determined by how many A's it had. For example, a 9A font would have proportionately more E's and M's than a 6A font.

A proof press is used for checking accuracy in typesetting. The printer would painstakingly set type one letter at a time in a galley, lock it in, ink the type, lay a sheet of paper on top, and run a heavy roller over it. From there it went to the proofreader. If all was correct, the galley went to the print department for the press run.

Dad had a printer run a box of sheets about the size of the Chicago Tribune folded horizontally. It was called the Chicago Page and was full of dummy stories with a blank spot near the top under a black bar with the word "EXTRA" emblazoned across it in white. The paper was newsprint, just like the real newspapers used.

A customer could say whatever he or she wanted in that blank area—as long as it fit. Because the type was a fixed size, only a certain number of letters could fit on a line. There were two lines, 25 letters and spaces each, no exceptions. It could be fudged a little if there were a lot of I's and no M's or W's, but 25 was the standard. Spaces between words had to be counted in the total.

Dad loved doing things fast; it upset him if a headline took more than 30 seconds from start to finish. He did the setup from right to left without ever looking at the rack of letters, slapped on some ink, slammed the paper down, ran the roller over it like a rocket sled on rails, and ripped the paper off to show to the customer. He was a lousy speller but he was never wrong. If the customer complained that something was misspelled, Dad just told him, "That's the way it's spelled now."

There's no way of telling how many headlines we made over the years but it's probably in the hundreds of thousands. Customers would bring in old, yellowed copies to show us. Ned Kubicki, one of our more prolific headline customers, brought one in from 1961 that had two spelling errors in it. The method of printing our headlines changed but people always got a real kick out of seeing their name in print.

Lessons Learned

In the late 40s or early 50's, no one remembers for sure, Dad started to expand his horizons beyond the confines of his store. With Herb Borinstein, one of the Magic Masters, he formed the Riley-Borin Novelty Company. He may have been trying to rival Johnson Smith or just trying the mail order business on his own.

Alfred Johnson Smith started selling novelties and practical jokes in Australia and, after moving to the States, shipped his first mail order package from Chicago in 1914. Today Johnson Smith is the biggest shipper of novelty items in the world.

Riley-Borin never had that kind of success. Printed in black and white with more than fifty pages of drawings of items from suppliers such as SS Adams Company and Berland Magic, their catalog looked very similar to Johnson Smith's. They might have been wholesaling from them. They never could have had all that merchandise in the store. There is no record of how they got their catalog into people's hands or if they ever shipped an order. Dad never talked about it much and very few copies of the Riley-Borin catalog exist today.

A few years later, Dad bought the rights to an item called the Indian Mystery Stick, a notched wooden rod with a propeller at one end. The magician rubbed a small dowel rod over the notches and the propeller spun. With those rights came ten thousand unassembled units. At that time a young man name Don Wiberg became interested in magic and started hanging around the store. Looking for something for Don to do, Dad put him to work putting the sticks together at five cents per assembled stick. The propeller was attached to the Mystery Stick by a screw, but the pre-drilled hole was too small and the stick split when the screw was inserted. Before Don could begin any assembly he had to drill out the hole to make it bigger. This was very time-consuming. Fortunately for Don, he was taking wood shop at Harper High School where his teacher showed him how to clamp the sticks between two slotted boards. That allowed him to drill twenty-five sticks in rapid succession. The next time Don came to work he went into the back room and quickly brought out a batch of assembled sticks. A few minutes later he brought out another batch and another a few minutes after that. Dad began to wonder who he had working with him back there. Realizing that Don's piecework deal of five cents per unit was costing him about three dollars an hour, a princely rate in those days, he quickly put Don on minimum wage, which was seventy-five cents an hour.

Dad didn't stop with the Indian Mystery Stick as he bought the rights to more novelty items. These items had to be put together, too, but he never again paid piecework for their assembly.

Child Labor

I didn't work in the store at an early age but that didn't mean I couldn't help. Dad sold items called boxed gags. A boxed gag is a two-part joke with the setup on the cover and the punchline inside. Every now and then he'd bring home a bunch of the parts that comprise these things and we'd assemble them at the dining room table after supper. During the day that table was Mom's place for her sewing. She made capes, ties, and other costume accessories for the store. There were always patterns and material spread out on the table, chairs, and her small sewing table in the corner. But, no matter how big a mess she had, it was always cleared for supper. Dad had to have his evening meal ready promptly when he came home at 6:05.

There were many different designs of boxed gags but I especially remember three. One was a yellow box about two inches square and a half inch deep. In black print, the top said, "Delightful to Have, Fun to Lose." Inside, sitting on a square of cotton was a plastic cherry. Another was a black box of similar proportions. Its top had gold writing that said, "For Plain or Fancy Screwing." Inside were two tiny screwdrivers, one had two rhinestones glued to it. Finally, there was a box that read "Manhole Cover." Inside was a Kotex.

The jokes meant nothing to me but the point was that I had a job to do. We would sit at the table assembling the parts until they were all together. He'd bring them back to the store the next day where they were kept in a special box and brought out for certain customers. By today's standards, items like this would be considered mild but back then they were deemed "risque" and couldn't be left where children could see them.

During those years, there was once incident that stands out above any other. One day I stopped by the store on my way home from St. Dorothy's School and Dad tried to put me to work in a different way. Above the store were two floors of apartments that stretched from the alley to 79th Street and east toward St. Lawrence. I bet my parents knew most of the tenants.

They were especially friendly with a gentleman named Erik Anderson who lived on the Rhodes side. He was an elderly man who lived alone and my parents used to take care of him. To my young eyes he might have been a thousand years old. One day my parents were getting concerned because they hadn't seen him in a while. Phone calls and repeated pounding on his door brought no response. They wanted to get in but they didn't know if there was next of kin or how to get hold of them if there were. Dad was never one for waiting around. He wanted to get in there NOW. Then he got an idea.

All those apartments had garbage chutes that led to the basement. Each had a door in the kitchen and, for some reason, another in the hallway. Dad opened the hallway door and pushed open the one in the kitchen. Now he had a way in but they weren't very big doors and he surely wasn't going to fit. Then he spied me. I was wafer-thin and light as a feather. He didn't ask, he just lifted me up to the garbage chute door and told me to go through and open the apartment door once I got inside.

Now, I had a couple of problems with this: if I could fit through those doors I could fall down the chute, and, if I did make it through, there might be a dead guy in there. I raised such a fuss that people started coming out of their apartments to see what was going on. When Dad put me down I high-tailed out of there. I never found out how he got in and I didn't care.

By the way, there was a dead guy in there. Mr. Anderson left my parents some money in his will. It was immediately put to good use in the store.

Down The Loop

There were many mornings where Dad had to leave early to pick up merchandise for the store. I went with him a lot in the days before I started school, riding in the front seat of our emerald-green '46 or '51 Chevy. There were no laws restricting kids under a certain age to the back seat, no child safety seats, and no seat belts. I might have had to kneel or sit on a phone book to see over the door. If we had any conversations at all I sure don't remember.

What I do remember is watching the scenery change. There were no expressways so our journeys were on surface streets. We passed through the Stockyards, industrial areas, slums, and neighborhoods just like ours. There were vehicles of every description: modern cars, ancient cars, trucks, electric busses, street cars including the Green Hornet and the older Red Rocket, push carts, and horse-drawn wagons. We were watching the city change from the old ways to the new. It was happening right in front of us and we just enjoyed the trip.

Dad's driving philosophy was different from what I would later learn in drivers' ed. He actually believed that he did, in fact, own the road. If there was a slow-moving vehicle in front of him, his expression of choice was "Take an alley, ya farmer!" If someone behind blew his horn at him he yelled "Go scratch yer ass." When Mom was with she'd remind him to watch his language because I was in the back seat. His standard retort was that I'd have to learn to drive some time. Years later I was surprised to find those two phrases nowhere in "Rules of the Road".

When he said we were going "down the loop" he meant downtown Chicago. The Loop is officially the part of the business district inside the loop formed by the Chicago Transit Authority elevated tracks but it came to mean anywhere downtown.

We could be going to Lakeview Novelties in the Lakeview neighborhood, naturally, or E.O. Drane & Company. They carried a line of magic tricks called Enardoe (EODrane backwards). Though the company is long gone, their products are still available today.

My favorite place on one of these trips was McClurg's. A.C. McClurg & Co. was a publishing house on East Ontario Street. I never did figure out what we were doing there but he had his reasons and I loved going. The trip in the open freight elevator was a highlight, so was walking around on the old wooden floors. If they could talk they'd tell the story of countless footsteps and many cartloads of books, comics, and other paper products. Every floor was permeated with the smell of ancient wood and musty books.

As soon as we got to our floor I'd head for a window. It didn't matter which, every one offered a different vista: the North side, downtown, or the Lake. In Chicago, Lake Michigan is known simply as the Lake. Those windows actually opened, too, making the experience real. There was nothing to come between me the smells and sounds of the city. The stench from the Stockyards or the fresh breeze from the Lake combined with the cacophony of car horns, jack hammers, sirens, and the general roar of city life to create a multi-sense symphony that can't be duplicated in today's hermetically-sealed, antiseptic enclosures.

Of all these trips I especially looked forward to going to Berwyn. When he said we were going to Berwyn, he was talking about Irvin H. Raditz and Company at 7112 W. Roosevelt Road. Mr. Raditz and his wife, Cora, became very good friends with my parents, taking us out to dinner and a visit afterward to their home at least once a year. They eventually lived in a fancy house in one of the upper-class western suburbs but originally lived in an apartment above their store. Dad got an idea from this that would dominate the last third of his life.

Raditz & Co. was located on the south side of Roosevelt Road where the sun never shone. Its storefront, lit dimly by a few incandescent bulbs house in yellowed glass globes, had old wooden floors that hadn't seen a scrubbing in many a year and its dusty showcases were laden with every kind of merchandise piled together in a chaotic hodgepodge. Wigs, handmade by women working in the back room on a line of sewing machines, were displayed on antiquated mannequin heads. Tricks and jokes might share a case with hobbies, magic, or makeup. Taller shelving units held toys and larger magical illusions with no thought to keeping things categorized, yet Mr. Raditz made it work. We would pop in unannounced and have what we needed in a matter of minutes.

So what was my reason for enjoying this trip above all the others? Mr. and Mrs. Raditz could not have children. He even told my father that he would remember me in his will if I was named after him. Irvin Riley? I suppose I could have lived with that if a substantial sum of cash was involved, and if my Dad didn't put it into the store before I saw even one cent of it. The reason I loved going there was that Mr. Raditz would always give me something. Dad would protest but I never went home empty-handed.

Except for one item, everything else it lost in the mists of time and memory but I'll never forget the boat. He reached up on the shelf and handed me a model speedboat. It had a battery-powered motor, a steerable rudder, and was made of wood. Real wood! I prized that boat until it had an unfortunate mishap in my backyard wading pool.

I Liked It, Too

Every July we'd pack the old Chevy and head up to the WeLikeIt cottage for summer vacation. I loved having the back seat to myself and watching the scenery. Most of the trip was on U.S. 12 which was 95th Street in the city. It took us past steel mills in Chicago, refineries in Whiting, Indiana, and more steel mills in Gary. There was a prison along the way where I was always reminded that it's where bad boys go. As we passed the Indiana Dunes State Park, the scenery changed to sand dunes and pine forests, especially along the Red Arrow Highway in Michigan. At St. Joseph we turned east and headed to Dowagiac. It was obvious that we'd arrived in town because someone would always yell "I see the pink house." Someone must have had difficulty finding his house among all the other white clapboard residences so he painted it Obnoxious Pink. In later years I think astronauts could see it from space. All alone on a corner just past town was a gas station made of stones cemented together. That's where we turned left to head to the road that led to the cottage. Our road was two ruts that turned to the right just before the sand pit and brought us to the front door.

Mom hated bugs of any kind and the floor inside was an entomologist's delight. No matter how well the place had been sealed the previous year there was every kind of insect dead on the floor the following summer. If we were the first ones to arrive that year we had to wait outside while Dad swept the place clean and made sure there were no survivors lurking.

Once that was done he'd open the winter shutters which were plywood with those distinctive green shingles, hinged at the top and braced by a 2x4 against the wall. Then all the windows were opened and the breeze filled the place with country air.

There were railroad tracks a short distance to our west, just past the sand pit. I'd hear a distant whistle first, then the rumbling, and finally the hissing of steam. That's when I'd fly out the screen door to someone yelling, "Don't slam the (whap) door" and watch the giant iron horse locomotive go roaring by. It happened several times a day and I never got tired of it.

We usually shared the place with Tom and Mary Johnson and their kids, Mary Ellen, Tommy, and Patsy. The Johnsons lived in the second building south of the store on the east side of Rhodes. Dad and Tom Johnson were best friends who never met a beer they didn't like. They really love their beer, or anybody else's. One night at Keller's they decided to see just how many they'd had between them so they told Keller to leave their empties on the bar. The final tally for the two of them was fifty. This went on almost every night. So much for my college fund. Maybe that's what really happened to Mr. Anderson's money.

The Johnson kids were several years older than me so I was left to my own devices for fun when we weren't all doing something at the lake. Straight down the road that led to our front door, it connected back to the main road. Across that road was a farm house with a boy my age. Gene and I would pal around climbing trees and running through the fields.

One day I wanted to be like him and go barefoot. It was an oppressively hot day and I thought I'd be much cooler without my shoes. I probably didn't take more than three steps before my city foot met a country rock and split wide open. I still have the scar.

There was blood everywhere. Mom was hysterical but set about to keep me from bleeding out. I remember sitting on the sink crying as she pumped the water in an attempt to wash out the grit and stop the bleeding.

As we sat there the sky turned dark as a storm blew in from Lake Michigan. Though it was mid-afternoon, it was dark as night. Lightning punctuated the darkness, illuminating the countryside like a flash from a camera as thunder echoed off the rolling hills. I wasn't scared as much as fascinated and I quickly forgot about my bloody foot. It was probably this event that began my life-long interest in weather.

All good things must end. Dad got tired of all the work involved in opening and closing the place. Besides, the open road was calling. It was time to move on. The WeLikeIt cottage had spent almost 30 years as the place to go for weekends and summer vacations. In 1956 it was left to face its destiny.

In 1983 I was camping with my kids at Warren Dunes State Park and decided to see if I could find the place. It was only 30 miles or so away. We found Dowagiac and even that old stone gas station. The pink house was gone. Finding the cottage was a little more difficult because the area had changed so much. Our road now turned left instead of right, there were houses where the sand pit used to be, and the area that used to be open to the breeze was a forest. Grandma Riley had planted two trees of heaven in 1929. It looked like they'd done well. In an overgrown area, amid a pile of rubble, the only recognizable things we found were remnants of bedsprings and one of those green shingles.

Some things are better left to memory. Memories may fade but they don't end up as weed-choked piles of rotted wood and rusted metal.

Time to Move On

By 1956 it was time to leave Rhodes Ave. We would have loved to stay right where we were but the neighborhood was changing, and not for the better. The first order of business was to find a new place for the store, then buy a house nearby.

The search for a new store involved spending Sunday afternoons driving through business areas looking for places to rent. We went west on 79th and 87th Streets as far as Western, and north and south on Halsted, Racine, and Ashland. We even looked on Michigan Avenue, a.k.a. "the Av," in Roseland. When Dad saw a For Rent sign, he slammed on his brakes in the middle of traffic to look. If it had any potential he'd ask Mom to get the information while traffic piled up behind us. As other drivers angrily pulled around and honked their horns or yelled, he responded to each one with a hearty "Go scratch yer ass." I made myself as small as possible in the back seat, glad to be in a neighborhood where nobody knew me.

This went on Sunday after Sunday. If a location wasn't rejected for being too this or not enough that, calls were made during the week for more information. If that information wasn't a cause for rejection, we'd meet with the realtor and look the place over. Then it was rejected. Finally, we found a spot at 1057 W. 79th Street, about 17 blocks, or two and a half miles, west of Rhodes Ave.

The real estate office was directly across 79th street. Dad didn't get the best of receptions from the agent. He was a sophisticated, impeccably-dressed man in a homburg hat and a Chesterfield coat. When he found out that his prospective lessee was the owner of a "trick shop" he said he'd give him a year and he watched from his window all summer to see how long it took his new tenant to fail. By the time Halloween came around and he saw the crowds Riley's was attracting, he probably wondered why he didn't sign Dad to a longer lease.

The new home of Riley's Trick Shop was a brick L-shaped building with the longer end running south on Aberdeen to the alley. The short end went east on the south side of the street. We were in the eastern unit, sharing the building with an engineering firm and the local draft board.

Moving day was June 30, 1956. It was a hectic day as friends and relatives swarmed the store, hauling out showcases, shelves, and merchandise. They drove it down 79th Street in an open 8 x 12 trailer hitched to the back of the Chevy. The kids rode in the trailer, waving at their friends and enjoying the fresh air. After the final load was on the trailer Dad took one last look around the store, as empty as the day he moved in. He'd founded a successful business in front and began his married life in a small room in back. No one will ever know what he was thinking but, when he was satisfied every last thing was packed up and nothing was forgotten, he uttered words I would hear many times in my life. Without looking back he said, "Let's get the hell out of here." He wasn't big on sentiment.

The new store opened on July 2, 1956, but we still lived back on Rhodes. Dad hated commuting, so the search began to find a nearby place to live. In the meantime, he changed the store's closing time from 6 p.m. to 5:30 so he could still make it home for supper at 6:05. So we spent another string of Sundays trooping through house after house, some as far away as Roseland. But Dad wanted to be close to work and, when a nice bungalow at 7923 S. Aberdeen Street became available, he pounced. It was only 300 feet away from the store's front door. His commuting days were over. On a chilly March Sunday in 1957, we left Rhodes Avenue forever.

79th & Aberdeen

Be It Ever So Humble

There wasn't much to move on moving day, but Dad hired John Dunne and the Irish Movers to move it. There was plenty of help from friends and relatives too, so the job didn't take long at all. The empty moving van in the alley attracted a bunch of the neighborhood kids and I made some new friends right away. Inside, the party was getting started. There was plenty of food, laughter, singing, and, of course, beer. Sometime during the night someone opened a can of Schlitz that erupted and left a mark on the ceiling. The Riley house had been christened.

The festivities centered on the dining room table that the previous owners had left. This was not the small table we'd had in the apartment. That was now our kitchen table. This was a dining room table of epic proportions. It sat ten easily, twenty if they all liked each other. And this group must have really liked each other--they stayed well past 3 a.m.

I didn't see any of that. Even though moving day was a big event, I still had to hit the rack at my usual time. It didn't bother me, though. I was spending my first night in my very own room. It was awesome. I had my own closet and my toy shelf was where I could keep an eye on it instead of being in the hallway between the kitchen and living room as it was back in the apartment. My new room also had a door that opened on a porch that ran the entire width of the house. The porch was lined with windows that would swing open in warmer weather. With the party going on just a few feet away I slept blissfully, dreaming of summer nights with my porch door open and the warm breeze bringing in the sounds of the city.

That dream was shattered at five the next morning as I was awakened to the sound of "woof...woof...woof...woof" spaced five or ten seconds apart like some kind of canine Chinese water torture. After an hour of this I got up to look out my window and saw a brown cocker spaniel being ignored at the back door of the house next door, not a dozen feet from my window. I would wake up to this for years to come.

Since I was up, I figured I'd explore my new digs. If the pyramid of empty Schlitz cans on the dining room table was any indication, no one else would be stirring for a long time. My bedroom door led to a hall with my parents' room at the other end. The bathroom was on the right. It had the original fixtures including a bathtub with claw feet on it. All the doors had crystal knobs. There was another bedroom off the living room. This would be where Mom kept her sewing machine, patterns, and material. It had a door leading to a small screened porch in the front of the house.

A left turn from the hallway led to a kitchen that had enough room for our old table and a whole lot more. It had a pantry that was about the size of our old kitchen. A door led to the same back porch that my room opened up on. To the right was a door that led outside and it had one of those screen doors with the single long spring. It held lots of "whaps" in its future.

A mysterious door in the kitchen opened on a stairway that led to the attic. There wasn't much up there except for a few planks down the middle, and lots of insulation between the floor joists. The only light came from small windows at the front and back. An adult could stand easily in the center but the roof tapered quickly down to the eaves. It wouldn't be much use except for storing a few things. It wasn't heated so I didn't stay long.

Then there was the basement. At the bottom of the stairs was a room built of ancient, soot-stained 2x4's and 1x3's, real ones that actually measured up to their size. It was full of coal. The coal bin, as it was called, was kept full by a man who dumped a ton or two of coal in the middle of the street, shoveled it into a wheel barrow, and dumped it through a grimy window above the pile of black fuel, one barrow at a time. That was the fuel supply for the centerpiece of the basement, a huge cement boiler that circulated water through metal radiators to keep the house warm. It was fed by a hopper that put lumps of coal at a steady rate into the furnace. If we didn't fill the hopper before going to bed, we'd wake up to a very cold house. The only other room downstairs was a small root cellar in the front. It was a dark, dirty, dismal place.

The New Store

The author at the Aberdeen store, 1956

The storefront on 79th Street was nothing spectacular, just a thousand square feet or so with a small bathroom in the right rear corner. The front window faced north with a view of the Tally Ho Bar and Grill across the street. It was one solid sheet of glass, measuring 8 feet high by 15 wide, east to west, angling in toward the door. Painted across the top was a sign touting our "Comical and Adv. Newspaper Headlines." Listed on either side was just about everything else we sold: dice, magic, costumes, gifts, cards, gags, games, puzzles, etc. Inside was a riser on which Dad displayed an assortment of merchandise and a short wall behind that where he put signs and other flat merchandise. Every square inch was packed with items placed in no particular order. He took great pride in his window display and changed it often.

He once gave the task of changing the window display to an unwitting employee who spent hours meticulously laying crepe paper as a base, strategically placing each and every item for maximum effect. Dad was shocked at how few items he'd put in. He ripped everything out, including the paper and yelled, "We're selling stock, not crepe paper, get the hell out of here." No one ever touched that window again.

There was one time when Don Wiberg asked if he could have a go at the window. It was New Year's Eve. Don removed everything and left a few party horns and hats around a pile of fake puke with a few fake mice standing over it. Dad pretended to be mildly amused but filled the window with stock first thing January 2nd.

The inside of the store held the same showcases and shelves from Rhodes, but in reverse. The counters were on the left and the hat and costume shelves were on the right. A new addition was an "adult room" at the back of the sales area where all those boxed gags we'd assembled were displayed in locked showcases. The cover was off each box and it was next to the contents so the customer could see setup and the joke. The room was probably ten feet long by six feet wide. One evening there were two young women who were obviously having a good time. Their laughter could be heard throughout the store. They must have laughed so hard they couldn't control themselves. On the way out, they apologized for the puddles they'd left on the floor. You had to be 21 to enter and many a teenager tried to wangle his way in to see what forbidden delights it held. They thought that because the old man worked alone they could distract him and sneak in. He was way too smart for that.

Because Dad worked alone most days I'd stop by after school and in the summer to visit and help out a little. It was an added bonus when one of my friends or classmates from St. Sabina School or Leo High School came in. I was working in the "coolest store in town."

My favorite trick was a fake spider that hung over the counter. It was an ugly thing made of some kind of black material with brown fur and long, thin springs for legs. Fish line, which suspended it from the ceiling, led to a hook on one of the shelves behind the counter. When a customer was looking at something in the proper spot in the case, one of us would release the spider. Counterweights made it descend slowly, just like the real thing. It worked especially well with women who would scream and head for the door or swat at it and send it flying.

The store on Rhodes had a wooden floor where Dad put one of Adams' items called a Floor Nickel. Just a standard U.S. Mint nickel soldered to a roofing nail, it had to be nailed carefully because an errant blow with a hammer would turn a thirty-five cent trick into a nickel and a nail. It could also be installed by drilling a pilot hole and forcing it in with your thumb. An unsuspecting customer attempting to grab it from the floor would be unable to move it. The new store had a cement floor so the floor nickel was not an option. Instead, he attached a dime to the underside of the top glass on the counter near the cash register. He used Elmer's glue because it dries clear. When giving change he'd say, "you dropped a dime" and the unwitting customer would make several passes at it before realizing he'd been had. That same dime was still in the case at our last location. It was joined in later years by a quarter because of inflation, but customers young and old still fell for it.

In the evenings he had Don Wiberg and Stan Grossman, who were members of the Magic Masters, helping out with the magic. It was fun to visit with them because Don loved wordplay and Stan was one of the quickest wits I ever knew. One night we were on the way home from a magic show downtown in one of the old Vaudeville houses and Stan was riding with us. As we passed a huge sign with what looked like a million light bulbs, I wondered aloud how much noise it would make if they all fell at the same time. Right away Stan said, "They can't fall, they're all light." I kept that and many of his other witticisms locked away for future use. They've served me well over the years.

Those two were always having fun at work. One time when we came home from vacation they'd filled the front window with our headlines reading "**UNDER NEW MANAGEMENT.**"

Dad used the touch method to make change. Without looking at the till, he picked up each coin by feel so he could keep an eye on the store at the same time. Don and Stan reveled in putting the coins in different compartments in the till. This drove Dad nuts. They also enjoyed stuffing the spring-loaded snakes from a can of Adams' Mixed Nuts into the till and watching the response when it flew out as a sale was rung up.

Stan has since passed away but Don is still doing magic. He has appeared on Bozo's Circus multiple times and has served as president of Magic Masters and the International Brotherhood of Magicians.

The Transformation

Almost from day one Dad started working on the basement. The wall of the coal bin nearest the front of the house was the staircase for our front door. Our front door wasn't actually on the front of the house but at the bottom of an eight-step staircase between our living room and dining room. It opened up on a sidewalk and a strip of grass that led to a mirror-image of our house next door. Built in 1917, both houses are still there.

The area to the front of the staircase was somewhat protected from the coal dust, so he started making it livable almost right away. The house was 40 years old and had an electrical system that definitely was not up to code. The light switches were push buttons. The top one was the ON button. Push it in to turn the lights on and the bottom, or OFF button, came out. The process was reversed to turn them off. Electricity ran through cloth-insulated wires. Dad's brother, Marty, came by a few times to show him how to fix it. Then he was on his own. He began by replacing the wiring. Then he replaced the two bare bulbs that were the only lighting in the basement with real lighting and outlets.

The store was open Monday and Thursday nights. He closed from 5:30 to 7 p.m. for supper and headed back to open until 9 p.m. On nights when the store wasn't open, he came home, scarfed down supper, and headed downstairs to work on the basement until the 10 o'clock news.

After some serious scrubbing, he had that front area looking good. He painted the walls a neutral color and the floor a brick red like his brother had in his basement. Then he moved our old sleeper sofa down from the living room, added a TV and a couple of chairs, and we had a cool place to watch ball games in the summer.

There were two problems: the brick-red paint flaked under foot traffic and dust from the coal bin got on everything.

The coal bin was an easy fix. On December 1, 1958, a man came with a sledge hammer to break up and haul away the old boiler. I remember the date because it was the same day as the tragic fire at Our Lady of Angels School. He carried all that cement out the basement door, took the coal hopper, the remaining coal, and even the old wood that was the coal bin. Dad probably paid him a few bucks extra to do that. That same man installed a new gas boiler. With a clean heating plant and the extra space provided by the removed coal bin, the basement transformation could begin in earnest.

The solution to the floor was more elusive. Dad tried gray paint but that flaked off as readily as the red. Then he had an idea. No one knows whether or not he thought of it himself but it was pure genius. He laid down a new coat of gray paint and, when it was dry, covered it with red, green, yellow, and blue dots. To that he added sprays of black. Now foot traffic was borne by the dots and the gray floor stayed intact. More than one visitor asked, "Where are the lines, Jim?" They thought it was tile.

He never painted that floor again. It lasted through countless parties, my friends playing on it almost every day, and a few floods. The Deep Tunnel Project was in its infancy then and the Chicago sewer system was notorious for backing up during heavy storms. The scraping of cues, as shuffleboard sticks are called, and the sliding of pucks had no impact on the floor either. We had a shuffleboard layout painted on the floor. It definitely wasn't regulation size, a Chicago bungalow didn't have the space for that, but it was lots of fun anyway.

In the area where the coal bin had been, he put a poker table. Its center was covered in green felt. Each of the eight positions had a tray for chips or coins and a holder on one side for a drink and an ashtray on the other. Many hands were played there amid clouds of cigar and cigarette smoke.

Dad's next big project was a bathroom. Built from knotty pine, it was nothing special, just a toilet and a sink. But it had one thing most bathrooms don't. Leaning in one corner was a wooden coffin that contained a store mannequin wrapped up like a mummy.

When that was finished he built a bar that would be the focal point of parties for years. It was an L-shape extending toward the back of the house from the fruit cellar and turning toward the north wall with the opening just before the wall. It had six stools. Behind the bar was a stainless steel sink like those found in commercial taverns. All those autographed pictures of magicians from the Rhodes store adorned the back wall. There was even a working vintage cash register with the pop-up numbers at the top. To keep his beer cold, he used the old refrigerator from the apartment on Rhodes.

The author, Jim Riley, and next-door neighbor Columbus DesChatelets behind the bar, 1959.

Some of the amenities for the bar were procured by Dad's friend Tom Johnson. Tom was a cigar salesman who had contacts all over town. There were many Sunday mornings when Dad and I made the trip to their house at 93rd and Racine to get "stuff." We'd head out from there to acquire all kinds of items. Some things came with home with us, others stayed with the Johnsons.

One time in particular we headed to Calumet City, Illinois, to some dingy warehouse in a less-than-savory neighborhood where we were met at a side door by some guy Tom knew. I was told to stay in the car while they loaded a heavy object wrapped in a mover's blanket in the trunk. For all I knew it could have been a body. Since we already had a coffin with a mummy in our basement, there wasn't much that would have surprised me. Back at the Johnson house they unwrapped a working slot machine. I don't know what would have happened to me had they been caught with contraband like that but I can guarantee Mom would not have been very pleased.

In the eight years we lived there, that basement saw its share of birthday parties, games of hide and seek, winter Saturdays racing model cars with my cousin Danny Malloy, lazy Sunday afternoons watching ball games, and overnight guests. We kids even invented the game of "Hoop It." Basically a game of tag, Hoop It required the kid who was "it" to wield a Hula Hoop. Whoever he or she hit with it was "it" and play continued. Somehow Hoop It never caught on anywhere else.

Bob Nelson, one of the original Magic Masters, had become Robin Nelson and toured the country with his traveling ice show, Jamboree On Ice. When he was in Chicago, our basement was his home and office.

The Magic Masters held their meetings in the basement for a few years, too. While the business part of the meeting was closed to non-members, I could go downstairs afterward to watch the guys show off their new effects. There's nothing like having a free magic show right in your own home. Many a prospective member waited nervously in our dining room while his fate was determined downstairs. After making his pitch to the membership he adjourned upstairs while the others voted him in or out. Voting was done using a wooden box with an opening in the top and a drawer in the bottom. The voter stuck his hand inside and deposited a marble in secret, white for yes or black for no. All it took was one black marble in the drawer for the newbie to be rejected, or black-balled. As far as I know, that never happened.

And so the basement that was once a dark, forbidding hole became a festive gathering place for family and friends.

Taking' Care of Business

Dad worked the store alone by day. Evenings and Saturdays, when it was a little busier, Stan Grossman or Don Wiberg came in to help. He worked six days a week. If he took a break for lunch he wolfed down a sandwich while standing at the counter. He wouldn't open on Sundays but many Sundays he went in right after Mass at St. Sabina's. We always walked to church and back together, no matter what the weather, but he would head toward the store do his paperwork when we got to 79th and Aberdeen. I continued home bearing the weight of the Sunday Tribune he'd bought in the church vestibule.

Things were going well during those years but the toll of working all those hours was catching up with him. More than once we had to rush him to St. George's Hospital. I was never told exactly what was the matter, but I know he had an ulcer and other digestive problems.

He never lost his spirit, though. Surgery was a lot more invasive back then and he lost his navel after one very intense trip to the OR. He thought it was hysterical and showed his lack of a belly-button to anyone who was interested, and probably many more who weren't. On a follow-up visit to the doctor, he used a theatrical adhesive called spirit gum, which he took from our makeup department, to attach a big red button from Mom's sewing supplies where his own belly-button should have been. Once the doctor composed himself he called all his colleagues, and people in the waiting room to see this miracle. That office visit lasted all afternoon.

Things always worked out for Dad. His cousin, Dan Malloy, moved his family to 78th and Throop and his wife, Ruth, came to work in the store. He was happy because some of the pressure was off him. Mom was happy because someone would be at the store with him in case he had any more health issues. I was ecstatic because their kids, Susan, Danny, and Janice would be within walking distance. We were great pals and now we'd see each other a lot more.

Dad was happy also because Dan Malloy would be a lot closer. They were more like brothers than cousins and could go round for round with the best of them, Dan with his Budweiser, Dad with his Schlitz. Now he could walk to a party at the Malloys' and not have to worry about how much he drank. We never had to count but it was pretty obvious when he'd had too much. He always wore a fedora in the winter, cocked at a rakish angle, the brim just above his eyes. The more he had to drink, the farther back on his head he put it as we headed home. That told Mom and me that we'd have to haul him out of at least one snowdrift before we got back to our house. Even if he was out partying on a work night, he still opened the store at the stroke of ten the next morning.

The Halloween business really took off during our years on 79th. The store hours were extended and, from October 15th to Halloween, he was open from 10 to 9 Monday through Friday with a supper break from 6 to 7 and 10 until 5:30 on Saturdays. He still would not open on Sunday. Mom was working overtime making costume accessories. Our dining room table was covered in capes, bow ties, clown hats, aprons, and other items in various stages of the construction process. When she got a call from the store that they were overwhelmed with customers, she grabbed anything that was ready for sale and went to help. If my homework was done I went, too.

It became so hectic at times that the store was crowded way beyond capacity and no one could move. Dan Malloy was drafted to work the door, letting in only a few customers at a time. This worked out much better for those in the store but probably not so well for other businesses on the block. Sometimes the line stretched all the way to Carpenter Street or around the corner on Aberdeen.

Halloween today is the second-biggest consumer holiday, right behind Christmas. Costume shops pop up in any empty storefront, carrying costumes of all types from traditional monsters to the latest movie characters. It wasn't like that back then. We didn't even sell full costumes. What costumes were available were flimsy plastic things sold in dime stores. We worked with a few suppliers that sold us masks, wigs, hats, and makeup. From that and Mom's accessories our customers had to use their imagination to make their costumes. Today there are hundreds of costume suppliers. You can get your entire costume all pre-packaged in a bag, no thought required.

I said Dad wouldn't open on Sundays. That's not entirely true. The original Chicago Saint Patrick's Day Parade got its start in our neighborhood and it came right past the store. March weather in the Midwest usually isn't conducive to standing outside for very long, so he opened the doors during the parade for friends and family to come in and get warm. Since the sun didn't reach our side of the street we sometimes had to stand on piles of snow to watch the parade. On one brutally cold day he took all the display items from the front window so we could watch from inside.

Parade participants gathered in Foster Park at 83rd and Loomis. The parade stepped off at 83rd and Ashland, went north to 79th Street, and headed east to Halsted. It seemed to last all afternoon as politicians and school bands paraded by. We even had an entry--a clown dressed as a Keystone Kop who carried a traffic sign that read, "STOP at Riley's" on one side and "GO to Riley's" on the other.

After the parade there was the obligatory party in our basement. I never knew I had so many relatives. Of course, there was plenty of food and the beer flowed freely. It didn't matter how late the party went or how much beer he'd consumed, Dad was always at the store at 10 a.m. the next day.

Tricks of the Trademarks

Dad had many different tricks he did over the years that were to become his trademarks.

He used to smoke cigars at work and one of his tricks was a sleight with his fingers that made it appear that he took the cigar out of his mouth and put the lit end back in. He amazed kids in the store with this trick for so long that they eventually brought their kids in to see it. One day he did it wrong and burned his mouth. He quit smoking shortly after.

When making change, he showed the customer the correct change in his open hand but held back a quarter by catching it with his thumb as the rest of the coins dropped into the customer's hand. The customer, satisfied that he'd been given the correct change, usually just dumped the coins in his pocket without a second thought. Dad could have been a richer man by keeping his mouth shut but he always told them what he'd done and to be careful in the future.

He had two favorites in restaurants: the bending spoon and the flying tablecloth.

During the course of a meal he'd tell the waitress that the silverware was very cheap in her restaurant. He then proceeded to bend the spoon until it apparently broke with a loud thud under his hands. Of course, he just appeared to bend the spoon. He let the end slip out from between his fingers and hit the table. Sometimes the response was shock but at one place the waitress said, "Everything's cheap here."

No one ever saw him do the tablecloth trick. That's the one where you grab the tablecloth and say you're going to whip it out from under the dishes and glasses without moving them. No one ever saw him do it because the restaurant staff would rush in to remove everything before he had the chance. At my cousin Sue's wedding, every server in the place ran to his table and cleared it in five seconds flat when he threatened to do it.

There were four gimmicks he carried with him wherever he went. He would eventually come to be known far and wide for them.

Many fell victim to a Dollar Snatcher, or what Dad called The Fast Buck. It's a spring-loaded reel with fish line to which you attach a dollar bill. When the line is stretched all the way you lay the dollar on the ground and hold the brake on the reel. As your victim approaches the dollar, you release the brake and the dollar flies back into your hand. His version was to ask someone if they'd ever seen a "fast buck." Holding the reel in one hand he pulled the dollar around his back in the other and "offer" it to his victim. When they reached for it, the dollar vanished.

He always carried a handkerchief, which was a perfect setup for an item called a Nose Blower. Also known as a Fart Whistle, it's a plastic tube with a short piece of flat rubber tubing attached. Blow into the tube hard enough and it makes a farting sound. He hid the blower in his hanky and blew into it as hard a possible while pretending to blow his nose. The resulting sound brought startled looks from around the room. He thought it hysterical. I wanted to fade into the wall.

He got the same response when he used the Snot Nose. Just a piece of silicone with a knot at one end that goes into the nose, it looks like a long string of snot hanging out. There was always one woman who would frantically reach into her purse for a Kleenex whenever he did this.

Sometimes he used the Snot Nose and the Nose Blower together in a prankster's pas de deux. He'd pretend to blow his nose. The Nose Blower got everyone's attention. When he'd pull the handkerchief away, the Snot Nose was there for all to see. No place or event was off limits. Weddings, birthdays, wakes, and family gatherings were fair game. I'm sure everyone at St. Sabina's was thankful he was a strict Catholic and refrained during Mass.

The Nose Pin was his favorite. An oversized safety pin appeared to be stuck through the wearer's nose. The picture says it all.

There was one trick that worked against him. One night our dog had thrown up in the hallway at the top of the basement stairs just as Dad was coming up.

I warned him about the mess as I went to get something to clean it up. He told me never to trick him with his own tricks. Fake puke had just been introduced by H. Fishlove and Company of Chicago. I warned him again, but he just told me to "get the hell out of here" and reached down to pick it up. As his hand slid into the gooey mess, he knew I wasn't fooling. With as much dignity as a hand full of whatever dogs throw up would allow, he headed to the bathroom across the hall with a strict warning not to tell anyone. As I wiped the mess up I did my best not to laugh as I made a mental list of who I was going to tell, and in what order. It was all over St. Sabina School the next day.

Wanderlust

Suppertime conversations in our house usually revolved around the store-- what Dad had done at work and how far Mom was with her sewing, but in January the conversations turned to vacation plans.

Because of the move to Aberdeen we stayed close to home in 1957 and did things around Chicago. The big thrill for me was going to my first baseball game. My prior experience with baseball was watching WGN as Jack Brickhouse called both Cubs and Sox games. I loved Ernie Banks and the Cubs and wanted to see a game at "beautiful Wrigley Field" but Dad was a Sox fan. We went to Comiskey Park instead. It didn't matter. I loved every part of watching big league baseball in person.

Dad was more impressed by the vendors. He loved how the beer man could open two bottles and pour them into plastic cups at the same time. The hot dog man was his favorite. You ordered your dog how you wanted it and the vendor added your relish, mustard, and ketchup as requested. Yes, they put ketchup on your hot dog. The Chicago ketchup ban wasn't in force in 1957. In one smooth motion he added your condiments as requested, wrapped your dog in wax paper, and sent it down the row. Anyone doing something quickly and smoothly without any wasted motion impressed Dad beyond measure. He probably watched the vendors more than the game.

By 1958 it was time to go beyond the horizon. We'd been to the Smoky Mountains and Mammoth Cave when we lived on Rhodes. We also took a trip around Lake Michigan before the Mackinac Bridge was finished. It was under construction and we could see the towers looming over the water but we had to wait four hours for a ferry to get us across the five-mile wide Straits of Mackinac. Today you can drive right across in just a few minutes with only one stop for a toll.

But now it was time to follow the advice of Horace Greeley and go west. In preparation, Dad traded in the '51 Chevy for a brand new 1958 Plymouth Savoy, a green two-door with huge tail fins. The Chicago Skyway opened shortly after and we took our new car to 79th and Stony Island to traverse this miracle of highway engineering on the day it opened. It was almost like flying as we soared above the rooftops on our short excursion to Whiting, Indiana, and back.

The big day came on a Sunday in July and we headed out right after the 6 a.m. Mass at St. Sabina. Oh, the wonders we saw on that trip: Dinosaur Park in Rapid City, South Dakota; The Corn Palace in Mitchell, South Dakota; Yellowstone, Zion, Bryce Canyon, and Grand Canyon National Parks; San Francisco, Los Angeles, and Disneyland. After seeing all that America had to offer, I wasn't as thrilled with Disneyland as I thought I'd be.

There was no Interstate Highway System then. That was a good thing because the essence of a road trip is lost when you can go from point A to point B on a sterile highway with only franchised restaurants and gas stations to keep you and your vehicle moving. The interstate system is great for getting from here to there quickly but you really don't see anything. That observation was first made by John Steinbeck in "Travels With Charley" and echoed by Charles Kuralt in his "On the Road" series on CBS. Jack Kerouac probably would have said it in his classic book, "On The Road" if interstates had been around. These books are required reading for anyone longing to take the Great American Road Trip, as is any book by William Least Heat Moon. But I digress.

We made most of the trip on two-lane roads past cornfields and through the centers of countless long-forgotten towns. A four-lane stretch of road was cause for celebration. Since I had the back seat all to myself I could move from window to window depending on which side had the more interesting vista. It was on this trip that I came down with a Keroackian love for a road trip that I've never found the cure for. I still love a road trip and would much rather drive than fly.

I wasn't just a passenger on this trip. Dad had taught me how to read a road map: red lines for major roads, blue lines for lesser roads, and grey lines for un-paved back roads. He even bought a device with a little wheel that rolled along those lines, with a meter like a one-handed clock face indicating the inches. Then he taught me how to use the number of inches measured and the legend on the map to figure distances. At the age of 9 I was entrusted with the duties of navigator for our cross-country adventure.

Another lesson I learned was that Dad was never off the clock, no matter how far he was from the store. As soon as we got into a motel room he moved the Gideon Bible out of the way to check the yellow pages to see if there was a novelty shop listed. If there was, it would be between Notaries-Public and Nurseries-Trees, Plants, Etc. The small towns where we usually spent the night had never even heard of a novelty shop, let alone have one. Some of the bigger towns did and we had to check them out right after supper. If the place was open we went in and looked around. If not, he'd peer through the window until the local police stopped to ask what he was doing. All he wanted to do was see if somebody was doing something better than he was. If so, the idea was implemented as soon as we got home.

We toured San Francisco with Al Lombardi, one of Dad's friends from the Chevaliers, and his family. In Riverside, California, we toured southern California with one of the Magic Masters, Frank Lopat, and his wife. On one journey they took us to Tijuana, Mexico. It was not the big deal it is today to cross the border. In fact, we drove right over it on the way back. It was after dark and we were stopped a few miles into California by a squad car whose flashing lights suddenly appeared out of the desert darkness. In a roadside interview by a flashlight shined into each of our faces they asked us where we were born. They must have been satisfied that we weren't illegal. They sent us on our way without even checking our ID's. Frank was born in Chile and made the mistake of telling them that on a prior visit. He had to go for an interrogation. This time, we told them we were all born in Chicago and we were on our way in minutes.

While in Tijuana, Mom bought a small bottle of Chanel No. 5 from a street vendor who guaranteed its authenticity, despite the low price, by showing her that the bottle was still sealed. When she got home she realized that she'd been had. Using a hypodermic syringe, the unscrupulous merchant had drained the Chanel and replaced it with water, leaving a bit of scent on the seal. Mom wrote him a letter of complaint. She wasn't expecting a response, she just wanted to vent. He actually wrote back. The issue was never resolved but he got on her correspondence list and they kept in touch for many years.

The next year we headed south to New Orleans and east to Florida. In Fort Lauderdale we hooked up with Nick Manola, who had owned the barber shop next to our store on Rhodes, and his family. We spent our days on the beach and nights on a huge tour boat going to some resort for dinner and a show.

One day we made a trip to Cape Canaveral to see how close we could get to the space center. America had only recently entered the space race and security was tight. Today it's no big deal to ride the causeway at the intersection of US 1 and Florida 405 to the cape. You can even bring a camera. In the summer of 1959 we were met at the gate at the mainland end of the causeway by armed GI's and told nicely, but firmly to leave.

1960's trip took us west on US 66, the "Mother Road" as it was called. I didn't realize it at the time but I was riding on a piece of American history that would soon by supplanted by the interstate system. Read John Steinbeck's "The Grapes of Wrath" for the significance of this highway.

In Missouri we began noticing small wooden cutouts of a rabbit on its haunches. On each was a distance: 1500 miles, 1400 miles, and so on. As the distance decreased, the size of the rabbit increased. After days of breathless anticipation as to what this wonder might be, we finally passed a rabbit sign indicating only one more mile. Somewhere in the panhandle of Texas we could see the giant rabbit ears in the distance. What was this place that had us looking for small rabbit signs for the last 1500 miles? The giant cutout rabbit sat on the roof on a junk/souvenir shop in an unpaved lot on the side of the road. You won't see **that** on the interstate. It was such a letdown we decided not to stop.

In those days, gas stations out west were few and far between. Most were privately owned and hadn't seen any sprucing up in decades. The horrors of their rest rooms is best left unspoken. Attendants pumped your gas, cleaned your glass, and checked your oil, radiator, battery, and air filter. The air filter sat on top of the motor and the cover was held on by a high-tech (for 1958) wingnut.

One attendant either didn't tighten it enough or forgot to replace it altogether. Later, as we headed up a mountain, there was a knock from the engine. Mom and I looked at each other quizzically but Dad instinctively checked the rear view mirror. Sure enough, the air filter cover was rolling back down the mountain to its final resting place at the bottom of some ravine. Now gravity was the only thing holding the air filter in place and we didn't want to lose that, too.

We had no idea when we'd find a Plymouth dealer so Dad stopped in the next town, got a wingnut from a hardware store and a tin pie plate from the grocery. One small hole in the pie plate later, the wingnut held it, and the air filter, firmly in place and we were on our way. It worked so well he didn't fix it until we got home. Every gas station attendant from there to California and back to Chicago asked him, "Whatcha cookin', Mister?"

In 1961 we took to the same road but in a new car, a beige four-door '61 Plymouth Belvedere with a slant six. This time we took Dad's sister, Mary, with us. She wanted to see some relatives in Torrence, California. Dad had no idea who these people were and referred to them as "my sister's relatives." On the way we toured Carlsbad Caverns. On the way back we spent a week in Denver.

That week in Denver saw a couple of firsts for us. We stayed in a hotel the entire time. Dad must have got a good deal on the room because he would never, ever spend that kind of money if he didn't have to. Maybe he got a good deal because Robin Nelson's Jamboree on Ice was playing in the club on the top floor and we knew the star. It was in Denver that I fell in love for the first time at the tender age of 12, almost 13.

Our days in Denver were spent touring the mountains. We visited the old mining town of Central City and panned for gold. In Colorado Springs we toured the Garden of the Gods, and drove up Pike's Peak at the blistering rate of 4 miles per hour. That was all the Plymouth could do in the rarefied air. Another day we walked out on the wood-planked span of the bridge over Royal Gorge and stared down at the Arkansas River a thousand feet below. Now the bridge is owned by Six Flags and they charge a king's ransom just to walk on it. Some days we just rode outside of town on US 6 and found a quiet place to sit and watch Clear Creek rush by.

On one trip we took a dirt road to some waterfall. The way in was against the mountain and the way out was on the canyon side. It was a very narrow gravel road without guardrails and the incoming and outgoing cars passed each other with the utmost caution. I found out why on the way out. Dad ordered Mom and me to switch seats. My job then was to lean my head out the front passenger window, watch the right front tire, and let him know how many inches he had before it went off the road. It was a long way to whatever river was down below.

Some evenings we watched Bob Nelson's show but others we went to visit Joe and Sadie Lombardo and their kids Nick and Kathy. I fell in love with Kathy, but she didn't appear to be interested. She was much older--fourteen, I think.

We left the country for our 1962 vacation. Our route took us up through Minnesota into Canada where we took a left turn at Kenora, Ontario, and followed Highway 1 all the way to Vancouver and, by ferry, to Vancouver Island. Anyone who thinks the plains of America are vast should head up north. Manitoba, Saskatchewan, and most of Alberta are endlessly flat farmland where the horizon seems to stretch to infinity.

As we pulled into Banff, Alberta, we had left the plains and were enjoying she splendor of the Canadian Rockies. Unfortunately, we were also seeing lots of **NO VACANCY** signs. It was the annual Calgary Stampede, a ten-day event in July that features rodeos, chuck wagon races, and many other events. It draws competitors and spectators from miles around and motels had been booked up months in advance. In the approaching darkness we saw a **VACANCY** sign but figured it must have been a mistake. There was no way this place could be fit for human habitation but we were running out of options. There was a light in the office and we got a room, for lack of a better word. It was a room in the sense that it had four walls, a floor, and a ceiling, but the beds looked like they hadn't been changed in a while and we shared a bathroom with another unit. The only divider between the rooms was something that looked like it might have been a shower curtain in its previous life. If there was any upside, the place was free of roaches. Even they wouldn't live there. Someone occupied the other unit but we never saw them. It's probably better that way. I wonder if they felt the same about us.

After a fitful night's sleep we went to the tourist bureau to see if anything better was available. There was, a friendly agent told us, just up the road in Jasper. "Just up the road" was 187 miles that we'd have to return on the next day to continue west. It turned out to be the highlight of the trip. Highway 93 took us through Banff and Jasper National Parks to a two-bedroom log cabin in a valley with a lake that reflected the mountains on each side. The cost was $12 Canadian. It even had a fully-stocked kitchen.

On the way back the next day we enjoyed the drive through the mountains again. We stopped at the Columbia Ice Field for a ride on the glacier in an eight-person vehicle with tracks for traction and skis for steering. In talking to our fellow passengers we found one person from Chicago who had been one of my Aunt Mary's students. This experience give credence to the main rule of a good road trip: a destination is a good thing but it's all about the journey.

Once back in the States we stopped for a few days in Seattle, staying with Bob Manola, who lived right on Puget Sound. He was the brother of Nick who owned the barber shop next to the Rhodes store. His brother, Joe, and his family lived next door. Just feet from his front door was a two-lane road with the beach just beyond. They had a speedboat that they let me drive. I never wanted to leave. We also visited Bonnie O'Toole and her family. The Space Needle was brand new that year and we made sure to visit that, too.

1963's adventure was Hawaii. This was not my first time in an airplane. That was a Cessna seaplane on Lake of the Ozarks near Bagnell Dam in Missouri. But it was my first time in a jet. Seeing all the places we'd been by car from 35,000 feet was awesome as was landing in San Francisco and Honolulu. That's where I got "leid" for the first time. This was a packaged tour with something going on every day including island-hopping in Hawaiian Airlines' fleet of DC-3's. We visited several islands, saw all the sights but there was still time to relax, enjoy the beach, and do some body-surfing.

One day as we were walking though the hotel lobby, Mom spotted Red Skelton looking in one of the shop windows. He was by himself, no entourage or bodyguards.

Richard (Red) Skelton was a star of stage, radio, and film and, at this time, had one of the highest rated TV shows, The Red Skelton Show, on CBS. He was a superstar in the truest sense of the word. He had to stand at least six-foot-two and was dressed in an outfit that looked one of the many characters from his show. His bright red hair peeked out from under a wide-brimmed hat. The fact that he was one of the era's biggest stars didn't deter Mom one bit. She walked all five-foot-nothing of right her up to him and asked if he would mind if she took his picture.

He turned to look at her, doffed his hat and said, "Yes, ma'am I would." But before Mom could react, he followed with, "The light in here is terrible, let's go outside." So, on the front steps of the Surfrider Hotel in Honolulu we got our picture taken with Red Skelton and had a nice visit until others realized who he was. Before long, he was mobbed. But he took it all in stride, shaking hands, posing for pictures, signing autographs, and doing some of his characters for anyone who asked. What a gentleman.

The summer of 1964 took us back to Canada. We turned east this time to Niagara Falls, Toronto, Montreal, and Quebec City. Reentering the country near Jackson, Maine, we headed for the Atlantic coast with stops in Boston and Philadelphia. This was a standard trip with no mishaps or outstanding events, just a tour of the historical sites in all the cities mentioned. On the way out of Philadelphia, Dad realized we had a few days left and, since we were so close to Washington, DC, we had another unplanned highlight.

We sat in the Senate gallery, visited our Senator's office, and saw all the monuments in a whirlwind one-day tour. On the way home our last stop was Gettysburg and a tour of the battlefield. I was 15 and knew about the Civil War from my history books but nothing brought it home like actually being where it happened.

This was our final trip in the Aberdeen years. I had been to at least 40 states by then and wanted to see more.

It's All About Characters

Any kind of business gets customers who don't fit into the standard demographic, but Riley's attracted way more than its fair share. These folks are drawn to magic and novelty stores like moths to a flame. Speaking of flames, there was one customer who would ask on every visit if it was hot in the store. He'd remove his hat and, using a cigarette, ignite a sheet of flash paper. Flash paper is treated with a chemical that makes the paper vanish in a quick burst of flame when exposed to a heat source. The inside of his hat was a testament to how many times he'd done that trick. Add in our "adult" room that offers things most stores don't carry and we got a mix of customers you won't find anywhere else. Factor in the show biz people Bob Nelson brought around and I've been exposed to so many different kinds of characters I thought they were all normal. There were two standouts on 79th Street, one named McDonald and the other, MacDonald.

To earn a couple of bucks every week to buy a pop at Drag's Delicatessen or get a new model car at Glider's Hobby Shop, I washed windows on the block between Aberdeen and Carpenter. That's how I got to know these characters.

Errol MacDonald was a 92-year-old wisp of a man, barely five feet tall and well south of 100 pounds. He still had a good supply of thick, white hair and his bony fingers were nicotine-stained from years of smoking unfiltered cigarettes. His early years were dedicated to the sea, working on steamers and sailing ships, but he was more than content to spend his remaining time living in the back of a store while repairing household items in front.

He hand-painted the gold-leaf sign on his window that identified his place as "The Studio." He named it that, he said, because "I didn't know how to spell 'emporium'." The studio was a collection of hand tools collected from far and wide, scattered the same way on various counter tops and workbenches. Like my mother, Mr. MacDonald made costume accessories for us.

When Dad sent me down there to pick up something, he knew I wouldn't be back any time soon. Like any good Irishman, Mr. MacDonald was an inveterate storyteller who loved to regale me with his tales of a life on the sea. I always remember the story of how he was in Halifax Harbor on December 6, 1917, when the Mont-Blanc, a French munitions ship, blew up. The blast damaged or destroyed 12,000 homes and took over 1900 lives.

Bob McDonald and his wife, Myrtle, aka Myrt, had another storefront a few doors away from The Studio where they sold pet care products under their own brand, Goody. They lived in the back where Bob made these concoctions himself. He tried making skin care products for human use but never could get any past the Food and Drug Administration. One of his products got me through my teen years. Put it on a zit and the zit was gone overnight.

Bob and Myrt talked constantly about nothing and everything all at once. He had a gravelly voice and took indecent liberties with the English language. Where most of us rinsed the dishes, he wrenched them. He called Mr. Raditz, Radish. The one that always got me was the word, poultice. In any dictionary, a poultice is soft, moist mass of bread, sugar, and other herbs applied as a treatment for the skin, like the ones my mother used on my cousin's boils. To him, a poultice was a batch of something as in, "I just made a poultice of stew, want some?" No, thank you, suddenly I'm not hungry.

Myrt had a heart of gold and could go word-for-word with Bob. Combine Zazu Pitts with Olive Oyl, add a pinch of Janis Joplin and you have an idea of how Myrt sounded. Try imagining her catchphrase, "Oh Bob, them are swell," in that voice. Now imagine listening to that over and over.

Granted, they'd survived the Great Depression but the McDonalds were as tight with a buck, or a penny, as anyone could be. He was getting on in years and put one gallon of gas at a time in his beat-up '57 Chevy station wagon. Gas was only 25 cents a gallon but his reasoning was that he didn't want to die with a full tank of gas.

One evening, my parents invited them to dinner with us at Jardine's in Tinley Park where they had an all-you-can-eat buffet. When they came back to the table, Bob and Myrt had piled their plates into a heaping mass of salad, meat, Jell-o, and everything else the buffet had to offer. Dad told them they could go back as many times as they wanted. Bob said, "We intend to." He then proceeded to dump their plates into a plastic bag and head back to the buffet.

This is not meant to be a put-down of anybody. It would be a very drab existence if we didn't come across characters to spice things up now and then.

The Times They Were A-Changin'

By the middle 60's there was change in the air; politically, racially, musically, and in just about every aspect of American society. It affected our little part of the world too. Because the black kids from Calumet High School went east from school to go home and the white guys from Leo went west, they had to pass each other on 79th Street at the end of the school day. The inevitable fights ensued. So the schools got together to change their dismissal times so the two groups could pass without seeing each other.

Dad had to close the store so the students from Calumet didn't come in and trash the place. One bad experience was enough for him. He locked the door for 45 minutes each afternoon until they'd all passed.

A bunch of us from Leo used to walk home down the alley, stopping between Carpenter and Aberdeen to recap the day's school activities and just hang out. The alley came to a T there, the top part going east and west, parallel with 79th Street. The bottom of the T went south toward 80th Street and beyond. We stopped there because I was the first one to leave the group. Then they headed on west to their respective homes and I went south a few doors down the alley to mine.

One day a group of guys coming down Carpenter from Calumet started harassing us. We would have fought them but there were way too many so we all ran to my house. It was the only safe place that was close. They chased us right to the back door but Chris, our dog, was there to save the day. With his mighty bark and teeth bared he charged all 35 pounds of himself into the yard and had those guys were jumping fences like Olympic athletes. From then on we decided to hang out in the basement.

The original plan was to start a Leo High School chess club but we couldn't afford more than one set of chessmen. I already had a checkerboard.

As a game of chess was going on, the rest watched or played with our table hockey game. One game of chess and one game of table hockey kept four guys occupied at a time. One day a couple of guys started dealing cards at the poker table. Before long, chess and table hockey were forgotten and we formed the Leo High School poker club. For some reason, the school wouldn't sanction it.

The neighborhood was changing and a black family moved in next door. What a blessing that was. The white people next to us, the ones with the dog that barked at their back door from five to seven every morning, would have a fit if I had any kids in the yard while they were taking their naps. It was all right for her mutt to wake everyone up at the crack of dawn but God help anyone who disturbed her afternoon nap, which she insisted on taking on her back porch. Our back porch was about four feet above ground and beneath it was dirt. We played marbles, cars, and anything else we could think of under there because it was nice and cool in the summer. It was a great place to build obstacles and run over them with our Remco Bulldog Tanks. Of course, we had to leave during her nap or she'd call the cops on us.

We got along great with our new neighbors. They had a bunch of kids so there was no problem about noise in our yard. Dad helped him fix his gutter one day and he returned the favor by bringing us barbecued ribs and chicken on Sunday. The old neighbors never did that. It was so nice having neighbors like these we thought we might be able to stay, but two incidents made us quickly change our minds.

One Friday night while Mom and Dad were watching TV in the basement and I was doing the same upstairs in the front room, I thought I heard voices outside. It sounded like a fight. Then I heard glass breaking. I turned off the light and the TV so I could see what was going on. A mob coming down Aberdeen from 80th Street, was breaking windows and trashing cars. As they got to the house to our south I saw a tall one heave a flagstone through the upper pane of the front window. It landed right where its owner, Mr. DesChatelets, had been sitting and probably would have killed him. They passed our house and headed to 79th Street.

When the police showed up they told us that the YMCA on 81st and Racine had held a dance to try and get the black and white kids to know each other. They called it a "Zebra dance" because they were trying to mix the black and whites. That may have been part of the problem. Tensions were running high and a riot ensued. He said what saved our house was that there were no lights on. They were targeting only the houses where it appeared someone was home.

Another night I was taking the garbage out to deposit into one of the city-provided 55-gallon drums that seemed to magically appear around election time. I heard a gunshot and almost instantly something hit our back fence. Whether I was targeted or it was just a random shot, there was no doubt about it, the time to move had come again.

Time to Move On, Part II

Now it was time to spend another bunch of Sundays cruising the main streets looking for a new home for Riley's Trick Shop. I had gone through driver's ed at Bogan High School and had my license by this time, but Dad insisted on driving. Once again I was relegated to the back seat as we scoured the storefronts seeking **FOR RENT** signs. Once again he'd slam on his brakes in the middle of the street when he saw one. Once again I got as low as I could in case anyone I knew was around. Once again he'd turn to the right and order Mom, "El, get that number" while turning to the left and yelling "Go scratch yer ass" to anyone who had the temerity to honk at him.

But the search proved fruitless. He was looking for something specific which just wasn't there. He wanted a store with a residence above like the Raditzes had had in Berwyn. The closest we came was a building at 99th and Kedzie, just across the street from Evergreen Park High School. That building became the Reilly Candy Company, which would lead to much confusion later on.

The search for the perfect building was going nowhere so he decided he'd build one himself. He really wanted to stay in Chicago so he pounced on a thirty by one hundred-foot lot at 9033 S. Western Ave. That set him back $8,000.

Wearing cheap cardboard top hats because Dad would never take a chance on something happening to any or our good ones, we broke ground on a clear, cold Sunday afternoon in March of 1965. In addition to the Malloys, several of the Chevaliers were there along with Harold Olson, one of the builders. That, of course, was followed by the mandatory party back in our basement on Aberdeen, one of the last we'd have there.

The headline reads "Friends Help The Rileys Break Ground March 14, 1965"

Harold Olson of Olson and Berklund Construction, oversaw the project. It went smoothly and we went there often to see how it was going. One morning, the bricklayers taught me a lesson that determined my choice of bedroom. The flexicore ceiling over the first floor had been installed and the guys were laying the bricks for the second floor. On climbing the ladder since the stairs weren't in yet, I noticed Mr. Olson and Mr. Burklund were working in the front of the building, happily taking their time to make sure that each and every brick was precisely laid with just the right amount of mortar between each row. It seemed strange to me that the two honchos would be doing grunt work like this themselves but they said they were enjoying the view. I responded that the view, which turned out to be the 14th tee at Beverly Country Club across Western Avenue, was indeed pretty nice. They directed my attention to a much closer view. As the light at 91st Street turned green I saw what they were talking about. We had an excellent view of women driving north on Western with their skirts hiked way up as they drove to work, offering much better scenery than the country club ever could. I decided then and there to take the front bedroom.

Construction continued apace as our final days on Aberdeen quickly approached. As they did, a family controversy arose, one that would rage for years. The official last day on 79th Street was scheduled for June 30, 1965, the day the lease expired. Dad put one of our newspaper headlines in the window that read: Closing July 1. Mom said it should read June 30 because that was the actual day of the closing. Dad's counter argument was that he didn't want people to think we wouldn't be there June 30. Mom's counter-counter argument was that people would think we would be open July 1, which we wouldn't.

I happily stayed out of this suppertime debate. The rejoinders flew fast and furious but I kept my mouth full at all times and excused myself as soon as I was finished eating. One night I didn't get out of there fast enough. As the argument reached its usual stalemate they both turned to me as asked what I thought. I didn't want to take sides but the best I could come up with was, "You can't close unless you open."

Mom sat back with the smug expression of the victor. Dad stormed off but not before yelling, "You always take her side." Actually, I didn't "always" take her side. It was just that she was almost always right.

This debate was far from over. Dad had to be right about everything, but now we had packing to do. Both the store and the house had to be moved in the same week and the store closing controversy had to simmer on the back burner.

It was bittersweet leaving the neighborhood where I grew up. There would be no more parties in the basement, no more picking Dad up out of the snow in the alley when he had too much to drink at the Malloys' house, no short walk to school or to mass at St. Sabina. One the other hand, most of my friends had already moved to other parts of the city and it wasn't safe to venture outside anymore.

So with the help of friends and relatives we packed up the house and the store and headed to Western Ave. As with the previous move, Dad rented a trailer and we had a good time riding up and down 79th Street in the back, waving farewell to all the places that had become so familiar: Dressel's Bakery, DesChatelet's Barber Shop, Highland Bowl, Monty's Tavern, Fasano's Pizza, Vito & Nick's Pizza, the Highland Theater, and White Castle.

One of Dad's customers was Earl Klier, the regional manager of the White Castle chain. He stopped by the store often and dropped off White Castle coupons with each visit. They were cut in the image of the Porcelain Palace, just like the box each burger came in, and were good for two sandwiches each. Dad didn't care for White Castles so he just kept amassing these coupons in a drawer. On moving day he told me to make sure the movers were fed, so my last visit to the White Castle at 79th and Loomis, one of my favorite hangouts, was to get 100 free sliders with the fifty coupons still in the drawer. Now, I'd used these coupons many times before but I guess fifty at one time was something rare for the Irish ladies at the counter. Bridgit, who had worked there 37 years according to her name tag, had to get the manager who gave me an inquisition as to the source of my bounty. Earl Klier's name was all he needed to hear. I got my 100 sliders in a matter of minutes.

As the last things were packed we took one final walk through 7923 S. Aberdeen, the only house my parents would ever own. Mom lamented the loss of her flower and vegetable gardens and her massive dining room table. As Dad took a last look at his miracle basement floor, the poker table, and the bar he'd built with his own hands, he turned and said, "Let's get the hell out of here."

Western Avenue

The New Digs

While the move to the new place went well, it took a little effort to get used to the changes. Our new home was smaller than the first floor of our house and there was no basement. Instead of eight steps up from ground level we now had fifteen. The back staircase was outside next to the gangway. It was metal and the stairs were diamond plate. Winter would be fun. On the plus side, we had our own place to park the car. Dad had always parked on the street, now he never had to worry about finding a space. And there was a double overhead garage door if he wanted to park inside. "I never pulled a car in a garage in my life, and I'm not about to start now," he said. "Besides, a garage is for stock, not cars."

Our dog, Chris, wasn't happy at all. He really missed his backyard. Outside the back door of the apartment was the top of the garage and he wouldn't do his business there. He hated going down the metal stairs, too. There wasn't much down there anyway, the gangway was nothing more than a sidewalk that was right up against the building next door. It ran from the front of the building to the back and was gated at each end. There was a strip of dirt maybe a foot wide next to our building. Not much would grow there because the sun reached it just a couple of days a year. Ryan's Woods was only a block north. He loved going there on our nightly walks and enjoyed sniffing everything along the way.

On Rhodes, Mom and Dad's bedroom looked out on the three-flat next door. On Aberdeen it opened on a gangway to the house next door, maybe six feet away. Here it looked out on the roof of the building housing Arthur Hamer and Associates, Certified Public Accountants.

My room overlooked the Beverly Country Club, as previously noted, but it also overlooked Western Avenue. Learning to sleep with all the traffic noise was a challenge. Mom and Dad hated air conditioning so we had to sleep with the windows open, even on the warmest nights. The breeze from the country club at least helped to keep the place cool. Even at night, the buses and trucks ran constantly, and the light at 91st was the starting line for many a drag race. High-powered street rods would rev their engines, taking off in a screech of tires as the light changed, their tires getting rubber as they slammed into second or third gear right under my window. But I learned to sleep through it all. The morning "scenery" was compensation for the nighttime noise.

Early one Sunday morning I woke up to something other than traffic. It appeared to be the paper boy, upset about having to bring a younger sibling on his route. In a pre-teen voice I heard, "Put the paper by the door, stooopid. Pick up the handle, stooopid. Pull the wagon, stooopid." This went on as far as I could hear. Apparently this was the only time the paper boy ever had a partner. I never heard it again.

In addition to the change of residence there was another change in the air. Mom didn't want me taking the CTA back into the old neighborhood. The distance was only three miles or so with a transfer at 79th and Western, but she wasn't happy about my having to stand out on the street alone waiting for the bus. She insisted that I transfer to Brother Rice. I told her in no uncertain terms that no self-respecting Leo man would even consider doing something like that. I won that argument and was able to maintain my dignity in addition to finishing high school with all my friends.

Through all this, Dad was happy as could be. He could go to work in any kind of weather without ever having to put on a coat. And, any time he got an idea about the store, he could go downstairs any time of the day or night and implement it. He did that often.

The new store was bigger than the one on 79th Street, twenty-five feet by seventy. The interior was laid out as on Rhodes with the counters to the right and hat cases to the left. There was a much larger "adult display room" as it was now called and lots more room for stock. The entire building was heated by a radiant system that was perfectly quiet except for the expansion and contraction of the pipes carrying the hot water through baseboard radiators in the apartment. The boiler was in the back of the store. The heat in the store came up through copper pipes in the cement floor.

The front display window was smaller than on 79th, maybe a foot and a half deep, ten feet wide, and three feet above the floor. There wasn't much foot traffic on Western but Dad still kept his window filled with merchandise. Since the building faced west, the afternoon sun was a problem. It would shine in our faces late in the day and fade the items on display. Dad always was a gadget freak and tried to fix that with an automated awning system. As the sun came around the front of the building it hit a light sensor that was supposed to run the motor that would lower the awning. "Supposed to" is the operative phrase. Most times it didn't work at all. When it did, the motor kept turning past the stop point and the canvas got caught up in the mechanism. It's a good thing we could do it manually. That was the only glitch and we settled into our new place, both upstairs and down, in no time.

Young shoppers leave their rides on the sidewalk.

Star Tracks

One unintended perk of moving to Western Avenue was our proximity to Drury Lane theatre on 95th Street in Evergreen Park. Drury Lane was a dinner theatre that hosted many B-list and former A-list stars like Pat O'Brien, Forrest Tucker, and Douglas Fairbanks, Jr. They performed in the round. The director was at our store at least once a week to buy props and makeup. He came in a beat up station wagon with Drury Lane's crest emblazoned on the side. For all the class and elegance Drury Lane exuded, they sure had a junky car with their name on it. He hooked us up with good seats and an occasional trip backstage to meet the performers.

One day I was printing newspaper headlines. Our press was up at the front window and I saw the old Drury Lane station wagon pull up. Thinking it was the director I went back to my work and waited for him to come in. When our front door opened, I turned around and was face to face with Tony Randall.

It was a few years before he would become a big star as Felix Unger in the Odd Couple but Tony Randall was still pretty well know from his TV and movie work. He also appeared many times with Johnny Carson on the Tonight Show where he resurrected old 20s and 30s songs. I was working alone and didn't know what to say but just said hello and treated him like a regular customer.

When my Aunt Ruth came back from lunch it was a different story. She made a very big deal when I told her that Tony Randall was in the store, but it could have turned sour when she when she asked him, "You're that guy who sings 'Tiptoe Through The Tulips', aren't you?"

He gave her a look of feigned indignation and said, "Oh, God no. That's Tiny Tim." He stayed an hour after that and entertained everyone who came in.

Louis Nye stopped in one Saturday afternoon while he was appearing at Drury Lane and Ernie Banks, Mr. Cub himself, paid us a visit once, too. That was just after his playing days. What a thrill for this Cub fan!

A Little Nonsense

Shortly after we opened on Western, a new conversation piece appeared on the front of our building, just to the left of the front door. It would greet visitors to our store from then on. Dad would never say where he heard the quote and it wasn't in any copy of *Bartlett's Familiar Quotations* available at the time. He never told us where he got the plaque or how much he paid either. He would be out there almost every day with his brass polish, keeping the message bright and shiny.

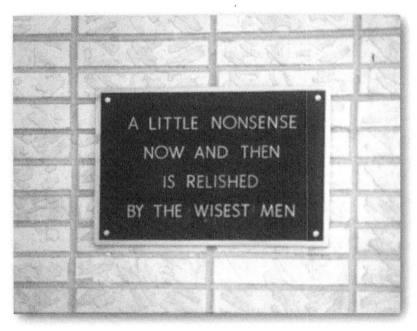

A LITTLE NONSENSE
NOW AND THEN
IS RELISHED
BY THE WISEST MEN

Years later I was watching the Willy Wonka movie for the umpteenth time with the kids and heard Gene Wilder utter the very same quote. It turned out that it was a line from Roald Dahl's 1964 book, *Charlie and the Chocolate Factory*. Where the Old Man got that quote will remain a mystery. He wasn't much of a reader and almost never went to the movies.

Sundays Will Never Be the Same

Dad worked in the store on Sunday mornings on 79th Street but he was normally home by noon after his paperwork was done. Then we'd head out to dinner at some restaurant if we didn't have someone's house to go to for a party. Mom was a good cook who hated cooking so we went out often. The Sunday dinner process could take the entire afternoon. We'd drive to some place and just get in the parking lot when one of them would note that it looked too crowded. One of them didn't have a taste for the next place. At the next restaurant someone would remind us that we'd just been there. And so it went. By the time we actually ate, we were ravenous. Our plates were clean and we never needed a doggie bag.

The new store was much bigger and required a lot more work. Dad and I went to 7 a.m. Mass at Christ the King at 93rd and Hamilton and he went to work as soon as we got back. There's no telling what he did; he didn't want to be disturbed. Some days he wouldn't come back upstairs until 7 p.m. Sunday afternoon dinner was out of the question.

It didn't matter to me. Everybody I knew had a driver's license so there was always someone to hang out with. Winter Sundays brought a bunch of kids to our house and we headed with our sleds and toboggans to Ryan's Woods for an afternoon on the big hill. The parking lot was always jammed so we'd walk the half mile from our place through the woods and under 87th Street via the equestrian underpass. Sundays in the fall were Leo High School football games at Stagg, Eckersall, or Gateley Stadiums; Soldier Field if we made the playoffs. I had no lack of things to do.

Mom was a different story. I took her shopping sometimes but she was left to her own devices most Sundays. Since she didn't go to church she spent most Sunday mornings taking care of her correspondence list. The rest of the day she wanted to do something else, but Dad was in charge and the store was his life.

One Sunday she'd had it and let him know it. He'd missed lunch and supper. She'd spent another Sunday alone and wasn't going to take it anymore.

He told her that some men golf and others fish, but the store was his hobby. If he wanted to spend all day Sunday in the store, that's what he was going to do and he wouldn't hear another word about it. And he didn't, at least for a little while.

More Tricks and Treats

The Halloween business skyrocketed on Western Ave. Mom was busy making her costume accessories and working the counter when necessary along with Dad and my Aunt Ruth. Dan Malloy worked the door when he could. This store was much bigger than the one on 79th Street but we still couldn't let it get so crowded that no one could move. I worked nights and Saturdays with the Malloy kids.

On 79th Street most of our customers were within walking distance. On Western there were a lot more people driving but we didn't have a parking lot and there were only two spaces in front of our building. We couldn't see where people parked because our two spaces were always full and it was hard to see past the faces pressed against the window.

After the first couple of busy days we heard from the accountant to the south and the doctor to the north that they were not happy about all the extra cars in their lots. There wasn't much we could do about it so they just chained off the entrances to their lots. When we could see out to the street we found that people were parking in the median and on the west side of Western, taking their chances crossing four lanes of traffic. We could only imagine how our neighbors on Claremont and Oakley must have felt about the extra traffic and all the cars parked on their streets on those October afternoons.

Believe it or not, those long hours of selling Halloween merchandise were the easy part of the season. Halloween required hours of studying catalogs, dealing with salesmen, placing orders, and getting everything organized, priced, and displayed when it came in. This process started in the late winter or early spring when the suppliers' catalogues came out and continued right up until October.

Trade shows were another part of the process. Since there were only about a dozen or so suppliers of novelties and costume merchandise at that time, there weren't enough of them to get a venue and have a show of their own. Instead they came twice a year to the Housewares Show. One was in January and there was almost always a snowstorm or a brutal cold spell. The other came in July, usually during a miserable heat wave. At different times they were held in the International Amphitheater at 43rd and Halsted or the old Navy Pier on the Lake. Navy Pier was not the major tourist attraction is it today. It was in a sorry state of disrepair. There were gaps in the roof and the wary buyer had to negotiate puddles or ice on the floors, depending on the season.

The Housewares Show was what its name implies. We had to walk past booth after booth of tools, kitchen gadgets, and everything else related to the household just to find our suppliers. They didn't get an area of their own and were spread throughout the place. Then we had to contend with the reps who were never satisfied with our orders, no matter how big. Dad loved this give and take. We normally got there early on Sunday morning and stayed until they closed. Sunday was Dad's only day off. He left there energized, knowing he got the best deals he could. Mom and I were just exhausted.

When everything came in, we had boxes piled for days as we got it all organized and ready to go.

To make finding things easier during the hectic hours of Halloween, every item on display had a number which corresponded to a specific storage drawer or location. It would have been chaos without that system. Dad was happiest when everything was done efficiently.

Dad was a hard worker but when it was time to go home, it was time to go home--even during Halloween. When it got close to 9 p.m. he started making announcements about how many minutes were left until closing time. Although he never told customers to "get the hell out of here," he probably came close on more than one occasion. One particularly busy evening it was almost half an hour past closing time and he announced that we wanted to get out of there. Some woman asked "where do you go?" like we lived under the counters. You know his response.

On the Road Again

We took three trips together in the Western Avenue years. The summer I graduated from high school, we took probably the best road trip ever. Dad had bought a new 1966 white four-door Plymouth Belvedere with a radio. Sure, it was only AM and had one speaker in the dashboard, but we'd never had a car radio before. He never wanted one of those "noise boxes" but he liked the car and the radio came with so he decided to live with it. He probably made the dealer give it to him for nothing. We also had our first air conditioner, an after-market behemoth that filled the area from the floor to the dashboard in the middle of the front seat. At least we wouldn't have to drive through Kansas with the windows open on a hot July day.

Our target for this trip was the four corners area where Colorado, Utah, New Mexico, and Arizona all touch. It's the only place in the country where a person can put one foot in each of two states and one hand in each of two other states at the same time. Yes, like countless others, we have pictures of each of us doing exactly that. No, I won't show them here.

This area is home to some of the lesser-known national parks such as Arches, Capitol Reef, and Mesa Verde. We visited all of them. Canyonlands had just opened that year and they tried to keep it as pristine as possible. Its roads were two ruts with no guard rails along its two thousand-foot drops. On the way out we stopped at Dead Horse Point which is arguably the most awesome vista in the entire country. As Mom and I took in the breathtaking view, Dad said, "We can't stand here all day looking at a hole in the ground. Let's get the hell out of here."

The following year's target was Alaska. We hit the road on July first and celebrated Independence Day at a rodeo in Devil's Fork, North Dakota. This was a real rodeo. We sat on our cars to watch the events, a hastily-erected post and barbed wire fence the only thing separating us from the bulls and broncs. Cowboys flew in to a small airport, took part in their events, and flew back out to another rodeo somewhere else in the state.

Montana was a blast. We visited Glacier National Park along Going to The Sun Road and took a boat trip on amid the towering peaks surrounding Lake McDonald. On the flatter roads the speed limit was posted as "reasonable and prudent" by day. So, if your 1966 Plymouth V-8 could reasonably and prudently do 110 miles per hour, no one was going to stop you. I loved having a driver's license.

We left Vancouver, British Columbia, aboard the Princess Pat just as the cannon fired from Stanley Park. The gun was fired every evening at exactly 9:00 p.m. so ships in the harbor could set their chronometers. On the way to Skagway we stopped at Ketchikan and Juneau. The capital of America's biggest state had streets of mud and wooden sidewalks. The saloons had swinging doors. It truly was America's last frontier. From Skagway we took a train over the Chilcoot Pass, the route of the gold seekers in the rush of 1898, to Carcross, Yukon, where we dined on moose meat.

Many of our fellow passengers wound up on Mom's correspondence list and stayed there for the rest of their lives.

The following summer we headed to Texas for our last trip together. It can't be classified as a road trip because it was a packaged tour where we flew out of O'Hare to Houston and were bused everywhere. We toured the Johnson Space Center, the Houston Astrodome, and the Alamo in San Antonio, among others. About the only excitement came in San Antonio which was infested with grasshoppers. They were everywhere. There were only two sounds: the popping of insect bodies as cars drove over them and the screaming of my mother. She let out a yell every time a grasshopper came near her, or about once every five seconds.

In 1969 I opted to stay home because I wanted to follow the Apollo 11 mission to the moon. Mom and Dad went to Ireland and Sweden with Dad's sister Mary and Mary and Tommy Johnson. Dad got to visit his ancestral home and Mom finally met her relatives in Sweden with whom she'd been corresponding for years. She spoke some Swedish and they spoke some English, so they got along fine. On one excursion in Ireland they got lost and Dad went to ask directions. When he knocked of the door of a nearby house, a woman answered the door, looked at him and said, "You're Mr. Riley from Riley's Trick Shop." He thought his fame had spread internationally but she turned out to be a Chicagoan who was visiting relatives.

He Had A Dream

When we returned from vacation in August of 1966 there was trouble in the air. Martin Luther King was marching for open housing in Marquette Park. There had already been riots and looting on the West Side and emotions were running high on the South Side.

One Sunday, Dr. King was to lead a march down 79th Street toward Bogan High School. Mom wanted to see him so we drove over there to wait at the White Castle on 79th and Pulaski. It wasn't pretty. Every car that had a black person in it was pelted with stones and racial epithets. There was a really bad feeling in the air and we just didn't want to stay. On the way back east on 79th we glimpsed Dr. King and his associates as we drove by. I'm sure they had already heard what awaited them when they got to Pulaski.

We sold all kinds of flags at that time including the Confederate stars and bars. The people in Marquette Park were buying those rebel flags by the dozen and we quickly ran out. They were clamoring for more but there was no time to wait for a shipment from the manufacturer. We weren't taking sides, we just wanted to make a buck.

Now that I had my driver's license Dad sent me all over town to pick up stock for the store. On that day he sent me to Raditz in Berwyn. Irv Raditz had passed away a few years prior but his protégé, Laddie, ran the place for Mrs. Raditz. Laddie, whose last name I never knew, said he had a couple of hundred rebel flags in stock and I could come for them right away.

It was a nice summer day so I headed down Harlem to Roosevelt Road, windows open, WLS or WCFL blasting on the radio.

The flags were twelve by fifteen inches and stapled to 3/8 inch dowel rods about two feet long. They normally came bundled in dozens wrapped in brown paper, twelve dozen to a box. All Laddie had was open stock so I just threw all two hundred flags in the back seat and was on my way.

I had noticed on the way to Berwyn that southbound traffic on Harlem was really slow, so I decided to head east on Roosevelt to Western and go south from there. As I happily rolled east with the windows down and the radio blasting, I noticed a few burned-out store fronts. Then I noticed whole blocks that were burned out. Somewhere past Pulaski at a stoplight I realized that I was in the middle of the area where the West Side riots had occurred. I also realized that I was the only white person around and that I was in a white car with all the windows open and two hundred rebel flags in full view in the back seat.

I turned off the radio, looked straight ahead and, when the light changed, I punched it and didn't stop until I got to Western.

The Eagle Has Landed

In addition to staying home to watch the Apollo moon mission while my parents went to Ireland and Sweden I wanted a taste of being on my own, plus I was in love. I'd met Judy Fajnor the previous fall at a Xavier College mixer in the Sabre Room. My parents were going to be gone three weeks and I was going to have the time of my life. For the first time ever there was going to be no schedule, no place to be at any particular time, and no one to answer to.

I crawled out of bed whenever I woke up, watched the Cubs on a small TV on the back deck while soaking up the July sun, and hosted a party every night. Once the word spread that there was a nightly party at Riley's, there were people coming from far and wide to the newly-christened party deck to celebrate with loud music, dancing, and games of Twister under the stars. Fortunately, there was someone I knew in each group and there never was any trouble. The place was never trashed and they always cleaned up after themselves. They were just grateful to have a place to party.

The weekend when Neil Armstrong and Buzz Aldrin landed on the moon there was no party. The landing on the moon was the greatest achievement in the history of mankind. I didn't want to miss any of it. I had two TV's set up so I could watch the landing and follow the Cubs at the same time. On Sunday July 20 as the time came for the astronauts to land, the Cubs game was halted and they played the radio transmissions between Houston and the lunar lander "Eagle" through the stadium's speakers. You could hear a pin drop. Then Neil Armstrong uttered those famous words, "Houston, Tranquility Base here. The Eagle has landed." Then Wrigley Field erupted. I did, too.

The next month, when the Apollo 11 crew came to town I went to the parade. I watched the crew go south on State Street then walked over to LaSalle to see them come north through a massive ticker tape parade. Finally, I worked my way into the thousands in Daley Plaza to hear them speak under the watchful eyes of the Picasso. What a great time to be alive.

My parents were scheduled to visit some friends in New York on their way back and be home on the 30th, so our final parties were the weekend of July 25 and 26. I had it all planned out. Garbage day would be on the 29th and all the evidence would be gone. One person does not make a whole lot of garbage, but parties every night of the week do. Our two 55-gallon drums were full to overflowing each week.

My Aunt Ruth died that weekend. She'd struggled with cancer for years and we knew she was very ill, but nobody expected the end would come so soon. I contacted my parents in New York and they immediately made plans to come home Monday evening. I had to scramble. I spent all day Monday filling the trunk of my '66 Falcon with cans and bottles, driving them to the garbage cans in Ryan's Woods. Then I had to go over the apartment with a fine-toothed comb to make sure nothing was out of place. I picked them up at O'Hare and they found the place just as they had left it.

One In A Million

Dad did not suffer fools gladly. This applied to customers and employees alike but employees took the brunt of it. Rare was the worker he really liked. Most he just tolerated and the rest he couldn't stand. He never had to say anything to them directly but they knew. More than one left in tears--especially the females. If he really liked a new hire, he took him or her under his wing and showed them how to be good employees. Bob Jaderberg, now a journalist, told us that he got his first job at Riley's and his work ethic from my Dad.

Riley's had hundreds of employees over the decades. Some lasted only a few hours, others for many years. Their stories could be uplifting or down-right heart-wrenching. Some kept in touch with us, others we never heard from again. One went on to work for Wheel of Fortune, another went to jail. A few left on extremely bad terms but most bade us a fond farewell after working part time during school and going on to better things. But only one, other than the three of us, worked at all of our locations.

Jim Wallace was a bartender and magician who started working for Dad after he returned from the Navy in World War II. He worked part time on Rhodes and Aberdeen, then came on full time on Western. An excellent close-up magician from his bartending days, he amazed customers for years with magical feats from card magic to multiplying billiard balls. He lived in Roseland with his wife Marj, who also worked for us, and his four kids. When he came on full-time in 1970, he moved his family to Evergreen Park so he could be closer to the store.

Dad was an excellent checkers player and Jim would challenge him when things were slow. This was back in the Rhodes store. Jim never even came close to winning. One day he saw an ad for book called "How to Win at Checkers." It cost all of twenty-five cents. Jim sent for it right away, studied it, practiced, and, when he thought he was ready, he challenged Dad. Using all the skills he picked up in the book, he was soundly defeated yet again. When he wrote the author to complain and get his money back, he received a short note that said there were no refunds and, besides, his quarter had already been spent. Jim and Dad never played checkers again.

Other than the checkerboard, Dad had a soft spot for Jim, giving him a job when times were tough and a place to sleep it off when he needed it. Jim repaid us by being a faithful employee and friend for many years. After the big snow of 1967, when our car was stuck in the alley for ten days, he helped me get back to college, His International Harvester Scout was one of the few vehicles able to navigate in the snow.

It was by Jim's insistence that we got into the button business. We were already selling pre-printed buttons from a company called Say It With Buttons, later to become SWIB Industries. Due to the popularity of nationalist pride, buttons like **IRISH POWER, POLISH POWER, CROATIAN POWER**, and many more were doing a brisk business. We were taking orders for custom buttons, too. They were processed for us by a company called Greenwood Enterprises in the back of a sporting goods shop in Mt. Greenwood. They later moved to Evergreen Park and became American Greenwood. Their minimum order was 100 pieces and it took a week or two to get them done.

But some customers wanted only one button and they wanted it now. So we bought a two and a quarter-inch manually-operated button machine from N.G. Slater of New York City and started making our own buttons. If customers had their own artwork or photograph printed to the correct size, all we had to do was cut it and assemble the button. Cutting is done with a circular blade that cuts the insert, or artwork, into a properly-sized circle, 2.62 inches in diameter for a 2.25-inch button.

To make a button, the operator places a shell, which is the metal front of the button, the printed insert, and a pre-cut piece of clear mylar, in that order, into the left bottom die, then presses them all together using a lever attached to the top die. They remain in the top die as it lifts up. Then a pinback is placed into the right bottom die. This is the back of the button with the pin attached. The bottom die is moved into position and the top die is pressed into it. Raise the lever and a completed button is in the bottom die. A good operator can assemble two or three buttons in the time it took to read this paragraph.

Since we had only large letters for our headlines, there was no way we could design and print a button to order. That is until Jim talked us into buying a Leroy lettering machine from a company called Keuffel & Esser. The Leroy is similar to a pantograph. It uses a hand scriber with a pen at one end and a tracer pin at the other that follows the groove of a letter etched into a template. Templates come in all sizes and fonts. When a letter is done, the next letter is lined up and traced. This continues until the job is done. Make a mistake and you have to start over. If this sounds tedious and time-consuming, it is. Jim loved doing things like this. He even got a template that made outlines of letters. Once all the letters were done he colored them with fine felt-tip pens. If the customer wanted multiple buttons, he had to repeat this process for each one.

Jim was very artistic and designed some beautiful buttons for us over the years.

The Real World

During my senior year at St. Joseph's College in Rensselaer, Indiana, I tried my hand at getting a job in the corporate world. I had majored in business management but took every computer class the school offered. They didn't offer a minor in that subject but I had enough credits for one if they had.

The school's IBM 1130 is laughable now but it was state of the art in the late 60s. There was no monitor, no onboard memory, and no keyboard. All programs and data had to be entered via punch cards, one line of code per card. Computer students had to carry their punch cards with them to and from the computer center, sometimes as many as a thousand cards or more. Since there was no software available (the term "software" had yet to be coined) students were charged with writing programs for the school's use as part of their classroom assignments. After writing and co-writing some of these programs, I thought I was pretty hot stuff and started looking for a computer job in corporate America.

In talking to various recruiters I quickly realized I wasn't the hotshot I thought I was. It seemed that most of these people were ex-military and were miles ahead of me in their knowledge of information technology (another term that had yet to be coined). I don't know if it was my glazed eyes or my slack-jawed blank stare when they started talking, but I never got a callback.

Eventually, I was promised something in computers by Metropolitan Life Insurance at 34th and Ashland. So much for promises. They offered me a job as a debit man at $150 a week, not great but more than anybody else offered. Actually, it was the only offer I got.

A debit is an area that belongs to one agent. Mine was from Artesian Avenue on the west, 35th Street on the south, Damen Avenue on the east, and 33rd Street along with parts of Archer Road on the north. Nobody else from Metropolitan could sell there. The debit man's job was to service the company's accounts in his area. That included selling insurance, taking care of claims, and making monthly collections of some ancient industrial policies that netted the company a whopping five cents a week. A few of those policies where written before 1910. At some of my stops I picked up a quarter or twenty cents every month.

After a couple of days with my manager I was sent out on my own. I had two thick books of accounts into which I entered the amounts I collected at each place, one page per client. I was to be at each account on a certain day of the week, the same week each month. At the top of each client's page were special instructions like "no later than noon," "go to back door," or "knock on basement window near sidewalk." My personal favorite was "go up back stairs of building to south, walk across roof, knock on third window from alley on building next door. See Mary." Sure enough, Mary was there with her quarter every month.

For some of these people the highlight of the month was their visit from the Metropolitan man. I worked in an ethnically mixed neighborhood and was treated to all kinds of culinary delights. The best were the fried zucchini flowers. The lady who made them said they were considered an aphrodisiac. Since I was still somewhat of a newlywed, I had a dozen of them but only eight worked by the time I got home. Other people had a shot and a beer set up for me. I don't know how I got home some nights.

While I liked the job and the people I dealt with, it was pretty obvious I was no insurance salesman. The home office was putting pressure on the agency manager and he was leaning on my unit manager who put the arm on me to get more production out of my debit. My immediate predecessor was the one who put all the names in those thick books. I hadn't added to them at all. So, when Dad offered me $200 a week to work for him, I jumped at the chance.

Within a year after I quit Metropolitan, the company paid up all those industrial policies and eliminated the debit system. They said it was a cost-cutting measure. I like to think it was because I did such a great job that no one could replace me.

The Next Generation

On January 2, 1971, I started full time at Riley's. That extra $50 a week came in handy since I had a wife and a daughter at that time. Judy and I married shortly after graduation and moved to Blue Island and a one-bedroom apart-ment at 12504 Fairview. Instead of taking I-57 into the city to get to work, I just had to drive the 30 or so blocks down Western Avenue. I could even go home for supper on our late nights.

Except for our bedroom set, everything was scrounged. Our kitchen set came from a moving sale. A swivel chair and pole lamp that had adorned my dorm room at St. Joe's now resided in our living room. Our first TV was a black and white Philco with a tilted picture tube. Still, life was good. We lived in the same building as Bob and Sandy Langland who Judy had known most of her life. Our first daughter, Colleen, arrived within the year.

My new job was pretty much what I'd done before: wait on the customers, do headlines, sweep, take out the garbage. But now I was keeping the books, paying bills, and doing payroll. One of the duties of keeping the books was taking care of the Cook County personal property tax which was a tax on possessions other than real estate. Real estate was already taxed enough.

The forms for this tax came out around August every year. Shortly after, we'd get a call from someone who said, "Dis is Phil." In high school and college I'd just hand the phone to Dad who said very little. He scribbled down a few notes, hung up the phone, and said nothing. Then it was my turn. When Phil, if that was his real name, called that year, I handled it. He told me to "write one check ta da Cook Counny collector for nine hunnert dollars an' anudder one for six hunnert dollars made out ta caish and sen it ta dis address." Of course, it was a post office box. I felt slimy for the rest of the day. This was my introduction to the machinations of "Crook" County politics.

The next year I called a lawyer who handled the entire thing for under two hundred dollars. When "Phil" called, I told him to go crawl back under his rock. The personal property tax was very unpopular and was repealed shortly after.

In addition to not having to deal with the paperwork and taxes, Dad got another bonus.

With me there, he didn't have to work six days a week. Granted, it really wasn't much of a bonus for him to work less since he never wanted to do anything else, but Mom was ecstatic. He could take her shopping during the week and he didn't have so much to do on Sundays. She had given up driving years before and needed him to take her places. It worked out well for both of them and they started doing a lot of things they'd foregone all those years.

Growing a Business

Everything was great on Western Avenue. In addition to the Halloween business growing exponentially, so did everything else. With Jim Wallace as full-time magician, the magic department was always crowded. There were magicians, amateur and professional, coming in and out every day to get supplies or just talk to Jim. Ed Shunk, a.k.a. Mystic Ed, showed up every Saturday morning right when we opened and hung around talking magic until two or three in the afternoon. He did this without fail for almost the next twenty years. Other magicians asked if he worked for us.

Kids came by bicycle from far and wide. They came from Beverly, Mount Greenwood, Evergreen Park, and Oak Lawn. The sidewalk in front of the store was twenty-five feet wide by ten feet deep and I once counted 29 bicycles in that area. They came mostly for tricks and jokes but wound up being fascinated by the magic. Jim put on a lot of impromptu shows in those days and he started more than one kid on the road to being a magician.

It was a much simpler time. There were only six channels on TV, no VCR's, no DVD's, no cell phones with their thousands of apps, and no gaming systems. Kids weren't bombarded by thousands of distractions. Getting on a bike and riding to a trick shop to buy a pile of fake poo or a disappearing handkerchief was a fun way to spend a summer afternoon.

The infamous adult room had doubled in size and was usually packed with customers. It was the place to go for items of an adult nature other than heading to a slimy adult book store in some seedy neighborhood. Most respectable people would rather come to us.

Business increased and it wasn't long before the store was overcrowded with stock. Every square inch of space was full. To make room, Dad took out his desk which sat opposite the adult room. It was an old roll-top beauty with pigeon holes across the top. He originally got it on Rhodes and had done his paperwork there for almost 35 years. Instead of moving it upstairs or trying to sell it, he took a circular saw to it and out it went. "There's no time for sentiment when you need room for stock. Get it the hell out of here," he said.

My workspace wasn't much more than an old Chicago Board of Education teacher's desk that my Uncle Dan had "acquired" for us. He worked for the Board of Ed and was able to make things magically appear. The desk was tucked in the back stockroom with just enough space for a small metal folding chair and a place to work. Since it was in the corner of the stockroom I considered that twenty square feet of space my "corner office." Not two feet above the desktop was another shelf with stock piled to the ceiling.

Something had to be done. Dad called Harold Olson and had him put a ten-foot addition on the back of the building. Not only did this add 25,000 cubic feet of storage space but it also got rid of the hated garage door. Now there was more wall space for stock.

There had been a gas space heater in the back of the old stockroom but Dad wanted it in the corner of the new area. "Gotta have more room for stock," he said, so he and Jim Wallace moved it to the new back corner, added ten feet of gas pipe and made the other connections. On a subsequent fire inspection the inspector saw that it had been moved and asked for the paperwork. Dad told him he did it himself and there was no paperwork.

"That's not safe," the inspector said. "It's gotta be done by a licensed contractor."

"What'll it take to make it safe?" Dad asked.

They agreed that fifty bucks would to the trick and the new addition was approved for occupancy. It didn't take long before it was packed front to back, side to side, and top to bottom with stock.

SOB

It's not what you think, although I've been called what you're thinking more than once. It stands for Son Of the Boss and can work for the son or against him.

There's the lucky SOB. He has the nicest car in the parking lot and the second best parking spot, right next to Dad. He's brought in after four years of partying at some elite school where his grades are paid for through a large endowment. He bypasses all the entry-level positions, getting a title of vice president of this or that, and a large, cushy office from which he can abuse all his underlings. He comes in when he wants, leaves when he's bored, and takes month-long vacations to all the hot spots.

On the other side is the poor SOB. He has to work his way through junior college where he takes whatever business courses they offer while flipping burgers at the local White Castle. When he starts at Daddy's company he sweeps floors, takes out the garbage, and is abused by other employees. He's the first one in and the last to leave. If he gets vacation time at all, it's after the rest of the staff have made their selections.

As for me, I wasn't the lucky SOB but I wasn't the poor one either. I sure didn't go to an elite school but at least it was paid for. I had that corner office, such as it was, but I didn't get the second-best parking spot. Jim and Dad took the two best spots because their cars were bigger. I was driving a '69 Camaro and was relegated to the third spot which required me to back in from the alley while trying to avoid Jim's bumper on my right and the telephone pole on my left. If Jim parked too far over and I complained, they both told me "too bad about ya," Dad's standard response for complaints of any kind.

Working with your father can be daunting for anyone. Working with mine could be a nightmare. Outside the store he was the life of the party, always joking around and performing his trademark gags. In the store he was all business, always doing something, rearranging this, moving that, looking for any way to keep busy. Out of the blue he'd yell at me "go get some whaddaya-callit." I had to immediately drop what I was doing, assess what he was working on, ascertain what "whaddayacallit" he needed, and get moving in under a second. If I didn't move fast enough I'd hear, "don't just stand there witchyer bare ass hanging out, move." Asking for more information or a clarification would result in another tongue lashing so I had to run and hope I brought the correct "whaddayacallit." If it wasn't, I was told to "get it the hell out of here and get me what I want." It was nerve-wracking at first but I quickly learned to think on my feet. Maybe the old man knew what he was doing.

The first thing any new employee learned about my Dad was that he was the absolute boss of his store. He was never wrong. He once accused me of leaving the lights on the night before. The fact that I'd had the entire day off didn't make any difference. It was my fault and that was that.

If he made a mistake, he thought it hysterical. In the early 70s, times had changed and we followed them. Old movies were back in style and their posters were all the rage. From front to back of the sales area our ceiling held posters from such cinematic masterpieces such as "Gone With The Wind" "Casablanca" and "Frankenstein." We also had a good assortment of black light posters. To go along with this mod trend we also sold stretch pop bottles. An artist took 16-oz glass bottles of Coke, Pepsi, and 7-Up and held them over a flame until they warmed up and stretched into elongated shapes. They were displayed on top of our counter.

Access to the top shelf of those counters was gained by lifting the top of the counter from the back. They were hinged on the front, the customer's side. When Dad was adding new items to that top shelf, he was always in a hurry and never looked to see what was on top of the counter. Those pop bottles would slide off, shattering into a million pieces. He'd laugh like it was the funniest thing that ever happened before yelling at me to "stop standing there wichyer bare ass hanging out. Go sweep that up." If I broke one of those bottles he'd yell like I'd just set the building on fire.

Such is the life of an SOB.

Time to Move Again

By 1972 it was becoming clear that the Western Avenue building wasn't going to be able to sustain Riley's growth. There was the parking issue and, for some reason, there was a perception that there was a growing crime problem in the neighborhood. Our nighttime business fell of substantially. Beverly is, and was, one of the safest neighborhoods in Chicago, but a customer's perception is the business's reality. Something had to be done.

So began another round of searching for a new place. I'm sure there was plenty of "El, get that number" and "Go scratch yer ass" during this process as there had been on previous store-hunting expeditions. Fortunately, I didn't have to hunker down in the back seat this time. I was on my own. Judy and I had moved to our first house, a nice tri-level at 16505 George Drive in Oak Forest and we were expecting our second child.

This search was different in another aspect, too. Dad didn't even look at a place to rent.

He wanted property to build his dream store exactly the way he wanted it. There had to be room to construct a big building with a big living area on top. And there had to be plenty of space for our own parking lot.

He didn't want to leave the city but there weren't any suitable lots available. What was available was prohibitively expensive, so he widened his search to Evergreen Park and Oak Lawn. Lots along 95th Street, Pulaski, or Cicero could run as much as $1000 a front foot in 1972, so a lot with two hundred feet parallel to the street could run upwards of $200,000. So they expanded their search even more and settled on a lot in Worth at 111th and Natchez.

Actually, it was two lots totaling about 17,000 square feet. The front footage was 116 and the east side tapered to 55 feet in back. Both lots were 200 feet deep. The reason for the taper was a railroad spur that led to a racetrack south of 111th Street east of Ridgeland Avenue back in the early 1900s. That's where Holy Sepulchre Cemetery is now. One of the houses on Nagle Avenue, to the east, sits way back on its lot not far from where ours ended. It used to be some kind of station or depot for the railroad.

In 1972, 111th Street was a two-lane street with diagonal parking, just like any small Midwestern town. There was a small tavern to our east, appropriately called the Little Inn. To our west, across Natchez was an old farmhouse which would soon be razed and replaced with a Bonanza Steakhouse.

Immediately to the west of our property was the gravel base for the Bonanza parking lot. It was there that we parked on a rainy November afternoon for our second ground breaking ceremony in eight years. There were still corn stalks standing on our lot as we turned a few shovels of dirt with the same gold-painted spade we'd used for the store on Western.

Once again, Dad tapped Harold Olson of Olson and Berklund to oversee the construction. This would be a much bigger job than Western Ave. Not only was the building going to be larger but they'd have to build us a 35-car parking lot. The building would be huge, four thousand square feet on the main floor and a two thousand square foot apartment above. And this time, both the front and rear stairways would be enclosed. We'd lost count of how many times people had come up the open back stairway on Western and rapped on our kitchen window at all hours of the day and night in search of a whoopee cushion or joy buzzer.

Construction continued all winter as we began getting things ready for moving from Western. The first concern was to sell the place. Our eventual buyer was a telemarketing business that sold vacation property. They wanted to put in a "boiler room" with dozens of phone lines. The original deal was for us to be out by May 1, but a few construction delays set that back by three weeks. Dad had to rent his own building for the rest of May. While we were preparing to move out, they were preparing to move in and had installed all their phone lines before we left.

Another problem was flooring for the Worth store. There was delay after delay from the tile installers. They never could give us an exact time for starting the job, so Dad decided to take things into his own hands. More specifically, it was my hands. He sent me over to do the job. I had never done any kind of tiling before, let alone four thousand square feet of it, but I didn't think it could be all that hard.

It wasn't long before I found out differently. It was the middle of May and 80 degrees outside. In the store it never got above 60, even with the doors open. The electricians were still installing the lights, so I had to work around them in the dark with a propane lantern as my only light.

Laying tile is pretty straightforward. Spread the adhesive with a trowel, making sure there are plenty of grooves. Lay the tile, alternating the pattern with each piece. It's as easy as can be. Doing it four thousand times while kneeling on a cold, cement floor in the dark is not. Over the next four days I learned what pain is, but I persevered and the job got done. Almost forty years later, that tile was still there but it would come back to hurt me again.

The heavy lifting for this move was handled by a crew provided by Tommy Johnson and a truck with a lift gate. As one of them backed the truck up to the side door, he got a little too close to the wall and took a two-foot long gouge out of the brand new brickwork. Since this was volunteer labor and Tommy was the son of his best friend, Dad didn't yell too much. The scar is still there today.

The move took almost a week because we not only had to move the store but we had to move my parents, too. After each day's work we finished with a visit to the Little Inn next door, probably the loudest bar I've ever been in.

On May 19, 1973, the Western Avenue era came to an end as Dad took a final walk through the workplace and home he'd built for himself and said, "Let's get the hell out of here." With those words he moved out of Chicago where he'd lived all of his 65 years.

111ᵗʰ Street in Worth

An Inauspicious Beginning

We had it all planned. The last of our stock and equipment was moved in on Saturday, May 19th. We were going to take the following week to get organized and have a grand opening on Tuesday, May 29ᵗʰ, after relaxing over the Memorial Day weekend. Robert Burns was right when he said, "the best laid plans of mice and men gang aft agley" because our plans went as "agley" as any plans possibly could.

The moving crew had put all the show cases in their permanent places. The angle iron we had meticulously taken apart on Western Avenue had already been fashioned into our stock shelves. We piled all the stock willy-nilly in a corner from which we planned to take our time getting it all organized and displayed. When we came in on Monday the 21st we found that rain from the weekend's thunderstorm had leaked through the roof right into that corner. Flat roofs and rain are a bad combination. We would learn that again and again over the next forty years. So we took everything and threw it on shelves wherever we could find space, to be organized later. Some things were too wet to keep. Items were thrown here and there, some not to be seen again for two years.

Because of the cold and wet we had to keep the doors open to get some air flow and warmth while we worked. Our parking lot had yet to be paved and was just gravel. Our electricity hadn't been turned on either. But we still had customers. Some were looking for something specific, others just wanted to "check it out." For those who wanted a particular item, we had to search our shelves and tear through boxes by flashlight while working around those who were just looking. Boxes were everywhere and so were customers. It was a blessing and a curse.

Even before the building was finished, Dad started printing business cards, signs, letterheads, rubber stamps, and other promotional items with our new address—6464 W. 111th. He was never one for checking things out ahead of time, but everything always worked out for him. Still, I asked him if he'd made sure that was our official address. "It's gotta be, Jim," he told me, "it's gotta be." This time it came back to bite him. When the final address came back as 6442 he quietly threw all that stuff out and just as quietly had it printed all over again.

As May turned to June we finally got the parking lot paved and electricity turned on. Most things were in their proper places and Riley's in Worth was officially in business.

Adventures in Retail: Love Story

As anyone who's ever dealt with the public is painfully aware, every time you open your door or answer the phone, adventure awaits. From here on, our narrative will be interspersed with such tales.

One of our very first customers in the new store was Brunhilda Angleburg, a tall, austere, unsmiling, Teutonic-looking woman who, she told us, was madly in love with one Harold J. Sawbuck (not their real names). We never saw him. She was interested in our headlines and proceeded to relate her story of how she'd met him through death. She'd lost her husband in an accident. We never did know how he lost his wife. She left with a headline that read **"HAROLD J. SAWBUCK I LOVE YOU."**

As the summer wore on she stopped by every couple of days for more headlines. **"HAROLD J. SAWBUCK, ONE IN A MILLION"** or **"HAROLD J. SAWBUCK HAS IRISH LUCK AND RUSSIAN POWER."** She never called him Harry, Hal, or even Harold, always Harold J. Sawbuck. She said she left them on his front door for him to see when he came home. Later she started buying cardboard shamrocks and other decorations to put on his garage door and balloons to tie to his fence.

Seasons change and so do feelings. One September day she came in looking more stern than normal, if that was possible. She bought no balloons, no shamrocks, just a headline that read **"FAREWELL HAROLD J. SAWBUCK."** He'd taken a job far away and was leaving immediately.

Did all those headlines, balloons, and shamrocks drive him away? Did she find someone else? We'll never know. We never saw her again.

The Evolution of T-shirt Printing: The Early Years

Since we were known far and wide for our custom-printed T-shirts, a large part of Riley's history revolves around them. We'll come back to this subject time and again as the technology improves. For now, we'll begin at the beginning

We'd tried adding T-shirts to our line at the Western Avenue store but that endeavor failed miserably. I'd made a few shirts for my friends and myself but not many more and that idea was quickly scrapped. So it was not without some trepidation that we tried it again on 111th Street. Customers kept insisting.

We bought another Hix HT-400 shirt press, the workhorse of the industry, two-inch flock iron-on letters and transfers from a company called Roach, and more transfers from another company called The Rat's Hole.

T-shirt transfers were printed with the same ink used in silk screening but the print was put on a parchment-like paper and allowed to dry. When heated in the press, the ink transferred to the shirt. At least that was the idea. There are four variables in transfer printing: temperature, pressure, dwell time, and type of transfer. Each had to be within a narrow tolerance. If not, the shirt would scorch or the transfer wouldn't transfer. If the first three variables were perfect, the fourth came in to play. Some transfers were cold peel, some were hot. That means that the transfer paper had to be allowed to cool before peeling or peeled hot as soon as it came off the press. If it was a cold peel that was peeled hot, some of the ink stuck to the paper and the shirt was ruined. If it was a hot peel that was allowed to cool, no power on heaven or earth would get that transfer paper off and the shirt was ruined. We ruined a lot of shirts.

Customers were able to choose from more than 100 different transfers that we had in stock. None could be customized and nothing could be added. Deletions could be done with scissors or an X-acto knife.

We did photo shirts in those days, too. A customer brought in a picture which we sent to a lab to be turned into a T-shirt transfer. After two weeks or so, we got the transfer back and put it on the customer's shirt, if the lab didn't forget to reverse the image for transferring. The same variables applied to photo transfers and we ruined a lot of those shirts, too.

The only way we could customize a shirt was with iron-on letters. That was fine if the customer didn't want to say a lot. But if he went on some kind of rant, the letters filled the shirt from top to bottom and side to side, if they fit at all.

Such was the state of the T-shirt art. Clearly, something had to be done to make it better but we'd have to wait until the computer age. We did the best we could with what we had.

Change We Needed To Believe In

After only two years in Worth it was apparent that we needed to make major changes in the layout of the entire property. These changes didn't come all at once but the planning started almost as soon as we'd settled in.

Our sign had to be moved right away. The architect, thinking our angled lot bordered a street even though no street appeared on the survey plat, put our sign at the far southeast corner of our property, apparently to be visible to traffic in all directions at an intersection that didn't exist. That put it a good sixty feet from our front door, looming twenty-four feet high over the Little Inn next door. More than one customer went in there, thinking it was our store. So we had to move it in front of our building.

The sign was a pair of hollow twelve-inch diameter iron poles supporting three four by eight-foot panels with fluorescent lighting inside. The top panel was our name, the middle advertised our headlines, and the third was a marquee with plastic letters that we changed with the seasons. A couple of years after the move to its new location, the sign blew down on a very windy day. Not only did we have to put it back up but we also had to remove one of the panels. There was a new limit to the height of signs in Worth and we exceeded it. We eliminated the panel touting our headlines because people, reading what they wanted to read, were coming in asking if we sold newspapers.

Our first alarm system was a source of continuous problems. It went off at random and we never knew what was going to happen. There was an obnoxious siren inside and outside the building and it sent an electronic alarm to the police.

One morning, Jim Wallace was coming in early and turned it off but the police still got the silent alarm. After an unpleasant encounter with several of Worth's finest, he never used his key again. Instead, he would knock on the back door and wait for one of us to open it. It didn't matter how long he had to wait or how bad the weather was, he refused to open the door himself. One time I was doing something and didn't hear him knock. He stood outside in a pouring rain for twenty minutes until I eventually heard him

Another time, during business hours, I was standing by the register counting some cash.

There were other employees in the store so I was really intent on what I was doing. I looked up only to be staring down the barrel of a large gun. A silent alarm had gone to the police station and they thought a robbery was in progress. It took a few minutes to identify myself and prove that I was not a robber. It took a little longer for my heart to slow down, but it took no time at all to remove that alarm and replace it with something more reliable.

The most obvious need was more space. Four thousand square feet just wasn't enough.

So Dad had Olson and Burklund add a thousand square feet to the back of the building. That gave us plenty of space to store Halloween costumes and Santa Suits before the season and freed up more space in the original part of the building. As we moved stock from the overcrowded front into this vast new area, we finally found the last item from the move from Western. It didn't take long, though, to fill up this space too, but we had to live with it. There was nowhere else to go. We had taken up every square inch of space we could build on.

The architect put our bathroom under the front stairs leading to the apartment. It was functional, but very small. That wasn't the problem. Our lunchroom used to be in the same area, behind a wall that was later removed. Invariably, the second we sat down to lunch, someone had to use the bathroom. We'd have to listen to the sound of their activities or breathe in their noxious fumes when they were done. The straw that broke the camel's back, though, was one afternoon when a woman took what appeared to be her grandson into the bathroom while I was eating. Not only did she leave the door open, but she kept extolling the glories of the nice poo he'd just taken. We immediately moved the lunchroom away from that area and eventually to the new addition.

Our T-shirt department was originally just to the right of the front door but it was very crowded in this area and we tripped over each other a lot. We fixed that by moving to the back right side of the sales area. Removing the lunchroom wall gave us a lot of extra room to move, and plenty of space to store shirts, transfers and letters. Unfortunately, it wasn't long before we needed a secure place to display our Halloween costumes and that corner filled the bill. So we headed back to our original spot.

By then we'd accumulated a few more printing machines and lots more shirt inventory. If it was tight before it was even more so now. I told Dad we had to do something. I was trying to plant the idea that I wanted to move back to the rear of the sales area but he took another approach. Before I had a chance to talk him out of it he had Olson and Burklund putting a small addition behind the T-shirt area for storage of shirts and letters. It was eighteen feet long and six feet wide but it sure freed up a lot of space out front.

The Penthouse

My parents relished their new home. The master bedroom alone was twice as big as their entire living space behind the store on Rhodes Avenue. It had a three hundred square foot balcony right out their front bedroom door. Mom's sewing room was just down the hall. At the back of the apartment was a huge open area that was the living room, rec room, and dining area all in one open, L-shaped space. Mom wanted a house but Dad still wanted to live above the store and this was as close as she was going to get.

She hated using the clothes drier so the first thing Dad did for her was build a clothesline so she could hang her laundry outside on the back roof of the store, which was about eight hundred square feet before he built the addition. She used another clothesline in the utility room during the winter. She also wanted to grow vegetables and Dad built her wooden planters on the back roof, too. They filled them with dirt I brought hand over hand in buckets up the side of the building.

The back roof had a wide-open view to the sky and they enjoyed sitting out in the fresh air watching airplanes approaching Midway Airport. There were lots of trees to look at, too. Past our parking lot they had a view of the Little Inn next door, across Nagle Avenue was Super Automatic Transmission with Lupe's Pizza beyond. All those buildings are gone. Across Ridgeland Avenue they had a view of Holy Sepulchre Cemetery, where Dad's parents were buried. After moving the store three times, he'd be asked by customers if he'd ever move again. He told them, "My next move will be across the street to Holy Sepulchre."

The same year we moved into the new store, the Magic Masters moved their Past Presidents' Banquet to the Lexington House in Hickory Hills. It was on a Friday evening in March or April every year. Dad usually sold ten tables or more to his friends and customers. That's one hundred tickets out of eight or nine hundred sold. He was the top ticket seller for many years and for years he invited these folks back to his home for a gathering after the show. There was plenty of room and those parties went on until the wee hours of the morning. It never mattered how late the party went, he was always behind the counter at ten the next morning.

On The Road Yet Again

Now that Dad had faith that I could run the business in his absence, he set out to see the world.

Their first adventure was Australia and New Zealand. They were gone for three weeks and toured both countries extensively. Sydney, Melbourne, Perth, Adelaide, and the Outback, they did it all. I was collecting beer cans at the time and Dad brought me back a nice selection. He'd emptied most of them himself. In every airport from Sydney to Chicago he had to explain why he was setting off the metal detectors with empty beer cans.

The next year they went to South America, even climbing to Machu Picchu. How many people in their seventh decade can claim to have done that?

Another year they went back to Sweden, this time to watch the sun go down. At the time of the summer solstice they were driven to a spot at the very northernmost part of the country, near the Arctic Ocean. There, the sun seems to be setting but, as it approaches the horizon, it rises again. They made this entire trek just to see that. They never were the type to spend their time at a fancy resort, sitting in the sun drinking pina coladas. They also spent some time with Mom's relatives in Goteborg.

As for Judy and me, our vacations were mostly going to her parents' farm near Wild Rose, Wisconsin. They originally lived in Chicago but had friends up there. On one trip one of their friends made them an offer they couldn't refuse: $8000 for an 80-acre farm and a house. The house was a disaster but they made the four-hour trip weekend after weekend and made the place livable. A year later they moved in.

In the bicentennial year of 1976, our daughter Kristen was three and Colleen almost six. We left them with Judy's mother and finally took a honeymoon. We left from Wild Rose on our anniversary and headed west. Our car was a 1975 Datsun B-210, yellow with black trim, a four-speed, no air conditioning, and an eight-foot CB antenna.

Judy had never driven stick. I taught her with the promise that she would drive only on the open road, running through the gears once when she took the wheel, coasting to a stop when she was finished. It was a great idea in theory. Every time she took the wheel we ran almost immediately into construction. She couldn't handle the stop-and-go traffic. I drove most of the way.

Judy had never been west of the Mississippi so this trip was a real eye-opener for her. I showed her all the national parks I'd visited on earlier trips with my parents. Our ultimate goal was Las Vegas where we spent a couple of nights in the old MGM Grand Hotel, played a few slots, and took in several shows.

We arrived late to one of the shows and lost our reserved seats. As I reached for my wallet, the maître d' said he'd see what he could do. When he saw me start to pull out a twenty, he said he thought he saw something right up front. As he was looking, I put back the twenty and gave him a single which he immediately stashed in his pocket as he led us to our seats. Not wanting to see him on the way out, I led Judy through the kitchen and out the back door.

Vacations would go on hold for the next few years. Our son, Jim, was born the following spring and another son, Ed, came in the fall of the following year. Our house in Oak Forest was getting too small for the two of us and three kids. When Judy told me she was expecting a fourth, we left Oak Forest and moved to our current home in Homer Glen.

ROLL THE PRESSES!

Our headline business really went on a roll at the Worth location. In addition to the regular customers coming in the door, we'd picked up a couple of wedding photographers who used headlines to show whose wedding it was and when it took place. The bride and groom would hold it in one of the group shots and it would read something like

WEDDING BELLS RING
FOR JOHN AND MARY
BIG DAY IS AUGUST 14, 1978

The biggest of these photographers was Fred Fox Studios who would order as many as two hundred copies a month.

The ink we used was poured on a glass plate and would stay open until we needed it.

"Open" means it didn't dry up or set until it was put in a thin layer on paper. It worked quite well until the mid-70s when there was decreasing use for this type of ink and it became impossible to find. We had to switch to an ink that stayed open on the plate but didn't dry as quickly.

That led to one of Dad's greatest inventions: the headline drying machine. Since we had to place headlines in a bag for the customer to take home right away, we needed something to set the ink or else it would smear. Talcum powder worked but it flew everywhere. Our headline press was in the front of the store next to the window. No one remembers what was there before but opposite the press he built a box into which the person doing the headline turned around and clipped it to a board. Talcum powder was applied using a soft makeup brush dipped into the powder reservoir below. Here's where Dad's idea came into play. He had hooked up an old torpedo-type vacuum cleaner to a switch on the board where the headline was clipped. When the ink was dry, the used powder was sucked off the headline using the vacuum's hose and brush attachment. It was noisy but effective. He was so proud of his work that he showed everyone who came in, whether they wanted a headline or not.

This process dulled the ink. Fred Fox Studios was used to shiny ink and didn't like the dull finish. Every headline of theirs had to be carefully taken from the press and hung up to dry. During busy wedding months, when Fox ordered two hundred copies or more, we had headlines hanging everywhere for days on end.

In the summer of '76, in the midst of the CB craze, I was approached by a man who said he represented a car wax company. He wanted to include an offer of a custom bumper sticker with each can of car wax and asked if we could do it. He said he figured most people would order their CB handle on the top line and the channel they monitored on the bottom line. He didn't expect to do more than a couple of hundred. We would ship directly to the customer. So we agreed on a price and waited for orders.

Our bumper stickers were just da-glo self-adhesive paper in red, orange, yellow or green. They really weren't meant for outdoor use but we were able to spray them with a UV inhibitor and sealer that made them last a month or so, depending on the weather. We couldn't use the powder dryer because the powder took the color right out of the paper. They had to be hung up to dry.

It wasn't long before a few orders trickled in. Then it became a stream that turned into a torrent. At one point we had a backlog of well over a thousand. Each one had to be printed and carefully hung up with the customer's information attached. When a Fred Fox order came in, we had bumper stickers and headlines hanging up everywhere. The car wax offer ended Labor Day weekend but it was almost October before we got the last bumper sticker on its way. I promised to think twice about any future projects like this.

It Was The Best of Times

In addition to CB radio and disco music, there were a lot of strange things going on. Maybe it was because we'd become adjusted to the high cost of gasoline, now at more than a dollar per gallon, or maybe it was just the general jubilation that the war in Vietnam had ended. The novelty business jumped on these fads with gusto.

Streaking had swept the nation. Sporting events and even the Oscars had their share of naked runners showing their stuff across fields and stages. That led the invention of streaking powder. Basically just generic talcum powder in a bottle with a shaker top, it was touted on the label as "all you wear."

Of course we sold mood rings and pet rocks, too. A mood ring, for those who don't remember or have tried to forget, indicated the wearer's state of mind based on body heat: blue for relaxed, green for normal, yellow for tense, black for dead, etc. The pet rock was a rock with artificial eyes attached and was sold in a box with straw and air holes. It made its designer a millionaire. We didn't do as well.

One item that did very well was the Paul Powell Shoebox. Paul Powell was Illinois Secretary of State of in the late 60s. His motto: "There's only one thing worse than a defeated politician, and that's a broke one." Though he never officially made more than $30,000 a year (decent money in those days), close to a million dollars in cash was found stuffed in brief cases and shoeboxes upon his death. It was the shoeboxes that made the news and were the topic of discussion for a long time. Some local wag came out with a replica and did quite well with it. Just a plain white shoebox lettered in green with dollar signs and the words "Paul Powell Shoebox," it flew off our shelves. Some customers said they were going to use them as gift boxes, others told us they just wanted to use a tainted piece of Illinois history for storage of baseball cards, comic books and, yes, money. This is the very essence of the novelty business. Strike while the fad is hot because it won't last long.

Presidential masks became very popular the 70s. The first and still most popular was the over-the-head Richard Nixon mask with its elongated nose. Made of soft vinyl by Cesar, Inc. of France, it led to caricature masks of every president since. Many people wore the Nixon mask with Arab garb and carried a gas can for Halloween after the oil embargo of 1973. For the 1976 election they came out with likenesses of both candidates, Jerry Ford and Jimmy Carter. The Ford mask was kind of blah, like the candidate, while the Carter mask flashed that famous tooth-filled smile.

While the masks themselves probably didn't have anything to do with the outcome of the election, they led to what we called the "mask poll." In every election year in which there were masks available for each candidate, the mask that sold best during Halloween predicted the winner of the election a few days later.

Jimmy Carter's smiling face was the best seller in 1976 but was handily outsold by the wrinkled visage of Ronald Reagan four years later. In 1992, Bill Clinton's jowly smile beat the extremely high forehead of George H.W. Bush. 2004's George W. Bush's almost life-like mask trounced the clueless expression of John Kerry. And Barack Obama outsold John McCain in 2008 by a margin of 3-1. The mask poll never failed.

By the 2012 election Cesar had been sold and the new owner did not produce the masks the same way. In future elections you'll have to rely on Gallup, CNN, or one of the many other polling services. The mask poll is now history.

The Glory Years

As the 70s became the 80s, the business started to grow exponentially. More than once we advertised for extra help. In 1980 almost fifty applicants vied for two positions. During 1983's economic downturn, hundreds of people, some with advanced degrees and resumes an inch thick, applied for a job that required them to sell fake dog poo. Things were tough in the real world but people still needed a laugh and we had all the business we could handle.

In the spring of 1980 a man parked a Winnebago next to the store and asked me to come and look at his Halloween line. We'd had many salesmen like this before. They showed up with masks or hand-sewn costumes they'd made in their basements. Most of it was junk which was thrown in bags in car trunks or back seats. It was high-pressure selling, too, almost threatening if we didn't buy. What this man had was different, so was his presentation.

His vehicle was modified to show his entire line of costume accessories on sliding panels that ran down one side, and dozens of costumes individually hung from a pipe rack on the other. His bed was over the driver's compartment and, other than a bathroom and small galley, the motor home was full of merchandise. He was on the road for six weeks showing his products to stores like ours. There was no pressure either.

Of course, we bought from him then and every Halloween since. The company is called Rubie's and is the giant of the costume industry. Now they have to bring their line of merchandise to the trade shows in several semis.

Their display is the biggest at the show. They get all the movie tie-ins, too. If you've ever bought a packaged Halloween costume, odds are it's one of theirs.

While we didn't get a big as Rubie's, Halloween in the 80s was spectacular for us. There were no more than a dozen stores in the Chicago area that sold a good selection of costuming material. Sure, the chain stores sold packaged costumes, but they were cheap plastic and mostly for kids. We catered to adults. They were the real power behind Halloween. They designed their own costumes using what they had at home and came to us for whatever they needed to make their costumes complete.

By late August or early September every square inch of space in our store was filled with masks, wigs, beards, makeup, and costume accessories such as devil horns, weapons, mouse ears, and cat tails. That's where that new addition really came in handy. Before we built it, my parents had to keep stock upstairs in their apartment.

Our extended hours for Halloween started on Columbus Day, the usual kickoff for the season, and went straight through to October 31. We were open from 10 a.m. until 9 p.m. but we were in early to prepare for the day and stayed late to clean up. Saturday hours were 10 to 5:30. We still closed on Sundays. We had to watch the Bears; the 80s were very good for them, too.

A typical weekday had the six of us full-timers behind the counter. Four part-timers filtered in as their school days ended. Evenings were much busier. Everyone worked on Saturday. We had ten people for seven counters. Each clerk worked only his or her counter, taking care of one person at a time. If that person wanted to think, the clerk moved on to the next customer. We talked only to the person whose belly was touching the counter. The other people in the store, four and five deep at times, were ignored until they made their way to the counter. It would get too confusing otherwise. The three other clerks who weren't working a counter jumped in when a clerk needed help. They also replenished inventory as needed. This included long walks to the rear stockroom or climbing ladders to move stock from the top shelves into the drawers below. This was how we spent the last three weeks of October every year.

Before we began selling full costumes, our average sale was under five dollars. At the end of the day when we cleared our registers, they showed the totals for the day in both dollars and number of sales. In the course of an average day we rang up two to three thousand sales averaging less than five dollars each, a good indication of how hard we had to work.

Our aggressive radio advertising may have been a contributing factor to our Halloween success. We were on WFYR, WKQX, and WIND several times a day. More than once I drove to the Prudential Building to go on WFYR with Fred Winston, their morning disk jockey. The first time I just thought I was getting a tour of the station and a chance to meet him. When he read our commercial and announced that I was in the studio, he suddenly shoved the microphone in my face. I had no clue what to say. I was more prepared on subsequent visits and we had some really good segments. Sometimes he'd clear twenty or more minutes for me.

After an interview with Bob Del Giorno on WKQX, a customer told me he came from Michigan just because he heard me on the air. He said he didn't know of any Halloween shops in his area and drove all the way to our store. Today there are probably dozens of pop-up costume shops between here and there. A pop-up store is one that appears in an empty storefront for the month of October and is gone on November first.

Once Halloween was over we'd take the staff out do a nice dinner. During the course of the busy days each of us would note the dumb questions we'd been asked, but never told anyone else. After dinner we'd pull out our notes and read them aloud. The questions got funnier and funnier after each round of drinks and, before long, we'd be asked to leave. We never went back to the same place twice.

Here are a few sample questions: "Do you have a smiling monkey mask?" "What color is your black makeup?" "Do cats wear bow ties?" "Gimme a skinhead and beard to match?" (How you match a beard to a bald head is beyond me.) "Between Groucho and Marx, which one wore the hat?" "Is your fake blood red?" Yes, they were long days indeed.

For Halloween 1983 I'd written a commercial for WFYR that involved a mad scientist, who sounded like Boris Karloff, talking to his assistant, Igor. I sent it to Bill Towery, a producer and DJ for WFYR, who did the voices and sound effects. It aired during October of that year and I got some nice comments on it from customers. That following spring it was nominated for a Windy Award. The Windy was presented for outstanding excellence in Chicago radio advertising. Judy and I went to a fancy dinner at the Hyatt Regency Chicago where we hobnobbed with local radio celebs like Larry Lujack and Wally Phillips. Our ad was played with three others in our category and was well received by the others at our table. Unfortunately, this is Chicago and you have to know somebody to get anything. Bill Towery was new to town and not very well-known. Nobody had the faintest idea who I was. At least I have a nice certificate and the memory of a wonderful night out.

1983 was our highest-grossing year for the month of October. Unfortunately, Dad and Jim Wallace had done the Halloween ordering and were more concerned about getting the place filled with stock than whether or not we could actually sell it all. They spent way more than we took in and we lost money. Some of the things we bought were still on our shelves five years later, not because it wasn't selling but because they'd bought so much.

The next year I took over ordering and cut way back, much to the chagrin of our suppliers. We're not in the business of making them wealthy. As we got closer to Halloween we still had stock on the shelves but nowhere near as much as the previous year. With three days left until Halloween, Jim Wallace pulled me aside and said, "See what you've done? We have nothing left to sell."

We did over $50,000 in those three days while working at full capacity. So much for having nothing to sell. In November we had nothing left to sell, but that's exactly the point. Empty shelves and a full bank account are two very good things.

But the writing was on the wall. Sears and K-Mart would go heavy into Halloween in the following years and things would never be the same. We did well but never as well as in 1983. We were still advertising heavily and we got a nice boost from some free publicity in 1984. There was a story in the Chicago Tribune that led to an interview on Channel 26, a radio interview with Clark Webber on WIND, and an in-store piece with Alan Kresheksy that appeared on Channel 7 news. But now there was some heavy-duty competition to contend with.

Evolution of T-shirt printing: Technology

Just after Halloween in 1980 we took a giant step in T-shirt printing. A company called Xpres from Charlotte, North Carolina, had modified a Mita copier to print images, reversed for transferring, on a special transfer paper. The process was called sublimation and it revolutionized the garment printing industry. Sublimation is the process of going from a solid to a gas without passing through the liquid phase. The printer stuck tiny charged pellets to the transfer paper which fed from a two-hundred-foot roll in the machine. The paper was light-sensitive and had to be kept in the dark at all times. When heated, the pellets melted and the toner inside became a gas that permeated the fibers of the shirt. When the heat was removed and the transfer paper peeled, the print was part of the shirt, not on top of it like iron-on transfers or silk-screening. It would never crack or peel in the dryer. It even stood up to bleach.

The Xpres machine, as we called it, printed in black, red, blue, and green, one color at a time. Each color came in a hopper that was filled from a bottle and put into the machine as needed. The machine had room for one hopper at a time. Multiple-color shirts and caps could be printed but that required transfers to be printed for each color. Each transfer had to be cut and pasted into position to make a full-color transfer. This was back when "cut and paste" meant using scissors and glue. The problem with this was that each transfer printed black, the color of the pellet, no matter what color toner we were using. Doing multiple color images required careful separation of different color prints or else we'd get a surprise when the peeled the transfer paper. We got a lot of surprises.

Another problem was setting up lettering for shirts. Jim Wallace did setups for us using the Leroy machine, but they were too small to fill a shirt. So we bought a copier that did enlargements. Because it would go only 200% at a time, we sometimes had to run the prints two and three times. We needed something better.

A year and a half after we got the Xpres machine I went to O'Hare Field to pick up a Linographics machine from the American Air Freight terminal. I drove right onto the field where the planes were parked, backed up to the dock and they loaded me up. There were no security issues getting in or out. There wasn't even a guard at the gate. Try that today.

A Linographics machine used fonts on a reel. Each reel was black with transparent letters. When the letter was lined up, the operator pressed a foot switch and the letter was exposed under bright light on photographic paper. The paper was moved, the next letter was lined up and exposed, and the process continued until the setup was done. This was a photographic process, so it had to be done under a red light in a darkroom that we'd built around our slop sink and water heater. The paper had to be set with a fixer before it could go back into the light.

Since the letters could be enlarged or reduced as needed, this process served us well for both T-shirts and buttons.

Another Stab at Mail Order

Once we had a handle on printing T-shirts efficiently we thought it time to expand our horizons. After his experience with the Riley-Borin Novelty Company, Dad didn't like the idea of printing another catalog. I didn't either. Catalogs are expensive and difficult to maintain. Instead, I promoted our products to those catalog companies that carry little household gadgets and other items you didn't know you needed.

I sent pictures of our T-shirts, caps, and buttons to about a dozen of these catalog houses, with pricing and a short history of our company. The deal was that we could take any design or idea from a customer, imprint it, and send it back to them. We received only one positive response but I won't mention the company. They're still in business. It started off very well but ended badly.

They were interested in the shirts and caps. Every few days we'd get a packet of orders in the mail. Each order told us what size and color item, what color print, what they wanted it to say and where to send it. A shipping label was included. Our name or any other information was not to be seen by the customer. Fair enough. We billed them for a month's worth of orders and were paid right away.

What a sweet deal it was. We could work on these orders at our leisure when things were slow in the store. It kept us busy and added another revenue stream to the business.

On the Road Again

My parents hit the road in a big way in 80s. Because of Dad's driving style they took a lot of packaged tours. Their 1980 trip took them on another cruise to Alaska on a more extensive visit than we took in 1967. The next year they saw some extremes: Florida and Iceland. They started 1982 off at the Tournament of Roses Parade and the Rose Bowl game on New Year's Day. Dad got his pocket picked at the game. Later that year they went to the Kentucky Derby. I'd asked them to put $2 on the long shot but they bet on the wrong horse. That nag won me $25.00.

Later they started taking "mystery" trips. A company called Discovery Tours would announce that a trip was upcoming but wouldn't say where it was going. The only clue they would give was if the trip involved flying. Most of the trips were by bus. On a visit to Branson, Missouri, Dad was invited on stage with Anita Bryant. He did all his trademark bits and stopped the show. They toured the space center in Huntsville, Alabama, and spent three days and nights on a Mississippi riverboat.

They made a lot of new friends on these trips. When a new trip was announced, everyone called my parents to see if they were going. If not, nobody else did either. With their pockets full of tricks and jokes, they were the life of the trip and everyone wanted to go with.

With our growing brood, travel was difficult and expensive but we made it work. Cramming six people into a car wasn't going to be fun so we borrowed a pop-up camper from our friends Sue and Paul Pfotenhauer and did a short trip around Lake Michigan in 1982. We had just bought a Pontiac Bonneville station wagon. That gave the kids lots of room because the girls sat in the back seat and the boys spread out blankets and pillows in the way back. That's what they called the area behind the back seat. All our luggage and coolers were in the camper.

It was a short trip but we visited Mackinac Island, then crossed the Mackinac Bridge and took a ride through the Soo Locks. One night we camped by the shore of Lake Huron and another night we were lulled to sleep by the roaring of Tahquamenon Falls.

What we didn't plan on was the weather. Even though it was August, it got very cold in the North Woods at night. Every morning someone would ask when we're getting up and the response was, "When I can't see my breath anymore."

The next year we bought a camper of our own and headed to Disney World. At one campground in rural Georgia, Judy was preparing to do a load of wash. Typical of the area, the washer was outside on the porch of the building housing the washrooms. When she looked into the washer she wasn't sure what she was looking at and called me over to see if what was in the bottom of the tub was a stick or a snake. It was moving so I told her it was definitely a snake. A couple of good ole' boys nearby heard that and they pushed me out the way, fighting over which of them was "gonna kill thet there snake." We camped at KOA's from then on.

The following summer we took the kids out west to the Four Corners area where we toured all the national parks and monuments I'd seen with my parents and taken Judy to a few years before. It was the first time any of us had experienced desert and mountain camping.

On a mountain near Royal Gorge, Colorado, a storm passed through and woke us all up. At 3 a.m. the clouds had left and we went outside to look at a sky that offered us the best view of the Milky Way any of us had ever seen. The stars seemed closed enough to touch.

In Montrose, Colorado, we were awakened just after dawn by people banging on camper doors saying, "You gotta see this." We sure did. Floating just over our heads were dozens of hot air balloons in every shape and style. Later, as we drove into the mountains of the Black Canyon we rode above them as they drifted through the valley below. That was our last long camping trip but we used the camper many times at Warren Dunes and other local camping areas.

1987 was the last we would all take together. Flying was way too expensive for all six of us so we boarded an Amtrak train at Union Station and went to Washington, DC. There we rented a car and toured all the monuments including the White House and the Capitol building. From there we drove to Gettysburg for a tour of the battlefield and on to New York City via Philadelphia with a stop to visit the Liberty Bell.

Our first day in New York was Sunday so we went to Mass at St. Patrick's Cathedral. Walking back to the hotel, we witnessed a mugging on Fifth Avenue. In all my trips I'd never seen a crime committed. The doorman at our hotel told me that happens all the time and to be careful when venturing out of the hotel. Despite that warning and an encounter with two guys who tried so scam us over a taxi ride, we managed to see the Statue of Liberty, Macy's, and the Empire State Building before heading back home.

While all this was going on I was taking trips on my own. The Palos Heights Recreation Department sponsored white water rafting trips that left on Friday night of Memorial Day weekend and returned early on Memorial Day. I made six trips between 1982 and 1987. We rode all night in a bus, rafted the Youghiogheny River in Pennsylvania on Saturday, stayed in a motel that night, and rafted the Cheat River in West Virginia on Sunday. From there we jumped on the bus and came right home.

I can't say which was more fun--the rafting or the ride to and from. The bus had room for 47 passengers but the trip was limited to 35. The extra seats were filled with coolers as was the aisle. It was a rolling party. We played games, told jokes, and sang most of the night. The Youghiogheny was a nice, entry-level ride with mostly class II and III rapids but the Cheat was a lot more challenging. Some of its rapids approached class V and VI, the highest rating.

It was on one of those rapids on the 1987 trip that I was thrown from the raft. When I came out in calmer water I found that my right leg had been ripped down to the muscle from the knee to the ankle by whatever underwater obstacle it had encountered. Of course, I had to get back in the raft and finish the trip. The Cheat canyon is no place to walk out of. Since we had to get back on the bus right after we finished rafting, I didn't get professional medical help until I got back home. By then the trauma had spread to my foot and it was swollen. The ER doc said he'd never seen a foot that many shades of purple. He couldn't close the wound because there was nothing left to stitch. He just poured peroxide on it and gave me some pills for the infection he knew would set in.

Surprisingly, it wasn't all that painful and I returned to work right away. The only stipulation was that I wear shorts all summer to give it air. No problem there. The wound finally closed around Labor Day. Every now and then I get a hankering to go rafting again but all I have to do it look at my "souvenir" of that last ride down the Cheat and the hankering goes away in a hurry.

The Computer Age

Inventory was getting to be a real problem. We carried an ever-expanding line of tricks and jokes from companies like SS Adams, Loftus Novelty, and the Franco-American Novelty Company. From those few box gags I'd helped assemble back in the 50s, our adult room had expanded to hundreds of them from Loftus and Franco, and more from Golden's Magic Wand, Inventex, Panoramic Sales, Arnold Freed, and Leister Game. Not counting magic and Halloween, we had to keep track of more than a thousand items from dozens of suppliers. Even though everything was in a specific place and each item was numbered to correspond with its location in inventory, our index card file just wasn't going to cut it anymore.

In 1984, Apple had come out with its 2c computer. Built like a laptop with an external monitor, the 2c sported a whopping 128 kilobytes of RAM and no onboard memory. Software was on a 5.25-inch floppy as were all data files. Once the computer was running, the operator loaded the software then removed the software disk and loaded the data disk. Backup disks were vital.

We spent the $1300 for the complete system and I was ready to put my college computer training to good use. Unfortunately, the programming language for this machine was Basic and I'd been trained in Fortran. With no time to learn a new programming language, it was going to be difficult to write all the software I wanted for this machine. Undaunted, I was able to cobble together a decent database program that allowed me to enter such things as the supplier name, our item number, their item number, cost, price, and other data that made ordering as easy as could be.

Instead of slogging through our card files trying to remember who carried what, I was able to come in on Monday and get all the ordering done in under an hour. I did an eyeball inventory to see what was low. Then, with a printout on green and white pin-fed paper of what else we bought from the suppliers whose items were low, I could quickly see what else we needed and place my order. By ordering early Monday I was able to get our inventory filled up for the coming weekend.

This worked great for about a year. Then I came in one Monday and everything changed. Dad was standing at the back door. This usually meant I'd screwed up somehow and he was ready to let me have it. That morning was different, he was smiling, but I still had an ominous feeling of foreboding. Without a word of greeting he said, "Look how much space I made."

He loved to spend his Sundays changing things around. We'd come in on Monday and nothing was where it had been on Saturday. Until we got used to the new arrangement he'd yell at us whenever we couldn't find something. Then he'd change it again. I'd told him that he couldn't do that under the new computerized system, everything had to remain where it was. He reluctantly agreed, but the stress of leaving things alone must have finally got to him.

The week before had been very busy and there were plenty of holes on our stock shelves. I'd planned to start filling them as soon as I got in. What I found was complete disaster. What he meant by how much space he'd made was that, starting at the back of the store, he'd pushed all the remaining inventory into the empty spaces that I'd planned to fill, effectively destroying the numbering system he created and rendering my computer inventory system useless. It would take months to undo what he'd done and there was no guarantee he wouldn't do it again.

Of course, I was outraged and let him know it. He couldn't understand why I wasn't overjoyed at all the new empty space and told me he was quitting. That lasted all of two days. After running the store for more than forty years, he wasn't going to give up that easily. We made an uneasy peace. I brought the 2c home where it spent its remaining days as a word processor and game platform.

Farewell, Gutenberg

By 1985 we'd been doing our newspaper headlines for 36 years pretty much the same way as Johannes Gutenberg did in the 1400s. We would have liked to continue doing them that way forever but the times were changing. The ink we'd been using for the prior nine years was being phased out and it was getting harder and harder to get replacement letters for our aging fonts. We had two presses. One was strictly for making headlines and the other for making signs. All the signs for our merchandise were made on that press.

Letters take a beating. They're constantly being moved from their cases to the press and back again. They're being slapped with ink brayers and having those heavy rollers dragged over them. It takes a toll. The lettering on our signs was made with metal letters which were getting a lot of scratches and gouges. Headlines were made with wooden letters which hold up better than metal, but even they were showing their age. Customers began to complain about the flaws in their print. So the search for other options began.

We weren't looking specifically for a computer system but that seemed to be the only choice, so we settled on a Leading Edge computer linked to a gigantic C Itoh nine-pin dot matrix printer. As on the Apple, this computer had no onboard memory. Headline setups had to be saved by removing the floppy disk with the software and replacing it with another floppy for memory. The system came with four fonts and a limited amount of sizing options. Since it was designed to run with pin-fed continuous paper, we had to make a special sleeve with pin feed holes to run our remaining stock of headline blanks.

The biggest change was the noise. The only sound our old press made was the sound of the ink being applied or the low rumble of the roller being pulled over the paper. The new one's print head sounded like thousands of angry cicadas in the store. No matter where anyone was in the building, it was obvious that someone was doing a headline.

A big plus to doing headlines this way was that they were dry as soon as they came out of the machine. Sadly, Dad had to retire his patented talcum powder headline drying invention. We also retired our headline drying rack and the drying clips that had been all over the store. Fred Fox headlines didn't have to sit around to dry. They went out the day an order was finished.

As our old headline stock was running out, I called the people who sold us the printer to get dimensions on new headline stock. I was told that the widest we could go was fifteen inches which would be a little narrower than our old stock but not a big deal. The big deal was that they didn't tell me to include the pin feeder strips in that measurement. They added half an inch on each side. When the papers came in, they wouldn't fit in the printer--all ten thousand of them. That was not a happy day. We had to modify our pin feeder sleeve and print the new headlines one at a time until they ran out.

We didn't part with Vandercook Press. It held place of honor in the back of the store, its quoins ready to lock the type in position and the letters above ready to be lined up into headlines again.

Halloween Gets Its Own Show

By the mid-80s, Halloween was becoming a major holiday and a lot more suppliers were turning up. Transworld Exhibitions, who ran the Housewares Show that we'd attended for years, held the inaugural Halloween Show at the Rosemont Expo Center in Rosemont, Illinois, in the spring of 1985. There were about fifty exhibitors and we were amazed at all the new things they had to show.

The convention center sat on the east side of River Road across from a farm. There was limited parking on ground level and more up a steep ramp to the roof of the building. In the following years a second floor was added to the building and parking was in unpaved lots across River Road. Convention attendees where shuttled to the center by bus. As the show grew, so did the expo center. It's now the Donald E. Stephens Convention Center and covers 840,000 square feet. When the Halloween and Party Show is in town, every square inch of exhibition space is full. The farm has been replaced with hotels and the parking lot is a multi-level monstrosity with a domed sky bridge connecting to the hotels and the convention center.

It's a long walk from the parking lot to the center and an even longer one back when schlepping bags of catalogs and samples. The walk inside the show can be arduous, too. Navigating the narrow aisles, jostling with other buyers, and listening to the suppliers' spiels for five or six hours make for a very long day. It's a total sensory overload trying to digest everything amid the noise from thousands of conversations and the occasional explosion or scream.

The Halloween Show's final assault on the senses is the "Dark Zone." That's where they display all the mechanical and electronic devices for haunted houses. Except for any illumination from the displays themselves, the room is totally dark. The visitor is treated to a life-like mannequin screaming while being electrocuted, another vomiting his guts out, and still others suffering all kinds of indignities imposed upon them by various devices of torture born of the twisted minds of their designers. The screaming, wailing, moaning, and shrieking are non-stop, as are the sparks and strobe lights. We had many local haunted houses leaving flyers at our store during Halloween. There was no need for us to go to any of them. The Dark Zone was all the haunted house we could handle. Sorry, the public is not invited to the Halloween Show, or the Dark Zone.

For a while we went to four shows a year. We still had to see our regular suppliers twice a year at the Housewares Show. Then there was the Gift Show at McCormick Place where we had to find a few suppliers of party favors and over-the-hill gifts amid the thousands of other supplies displaying every kind of gift item imaginable. Eventually, they all came to Rosemont where we got to see all our suppliers in one place at one show.

Up, Up and Away

For years we'd sent out to the Maple City Rubber Company of Norwalk, Ohio, for custom-printed balloons for our customers. Most balloon suppliers are located in that part of north central Ohio because it's the home of many tire manufacturers and the center of American rubber production. Maple City has been producing balloons since 1914. They can turn around a minimum order of five hundred printed balloons in as little as six days, but sometimes customers need fewer than five hundred and they need them NOW.

Enter the Sterling Rubber Company. Operating from a basement in Addison, Illinois, they had no minimum order and could have a job ready in a day. Before the big concern about balloons being damaging to the environment and dangerous to birds, balloons were a very hot commodity. Customers were renting up to six helium tanks a week and buying balloons by the case. The ability to get a short order of balloons printed very quickly was a big part of our balloon business expansion.

When Sterling Rubber approached us in the early summer of 1986 to ask if we were interested in buying them out, we jumped at the chance. After we struck a deal, I rented a trailer, hitched it to my Chevy S-10 Blazer, and headed up to Addison. The balloon printer weighed six hundred pounds and its base wasn't much lighter. The trailer had a ramp that I could roll the two pieces up with our hand truck. There was no way I was going to lift them into the Blazer. Once back at our store I had to navigate the Blazer and trailer through the narrow, rutted opening that construction on 111th Street had left me, and our customers, to get into our parking lot. We set up the machine in the back of the store using a block and tackle to set the printer on its base and Riley's Trick Shop was in the balloon printing business. The $15,000 price tag was a bargain. We made it back within a year.

Printing balloons is done via an offset process. The print is laid out reading left to right on a roller. As that roller spins, it picks up ink from an ink roller and then prints the design from right to left on a rubber roller. All the rollers are turning. The operator inflates a balloon using an air compressor and presses the balloon on the rubber roller, transferring the print to the balloon. The printed balloon is placed in a box to deflate. When all the balloons are printed, they're heated with a regular household blow drier to return them to their original shape.

The ink is rubber-based and must be mixed with two solvents in the proper proportion. Get the proportions wrong and the print is hardly visible on the balloon or it's too thick and smears on the other balloons in the box while deflating. It sure seemed easy when they showed me at Sterling Rubber. Back at our place it was a different story. I could never get the ratios right. It was the first time I'd regretted dropping chemistry in high school.

One of the girls working for us offered to give it a shot and it worked for her. She could mix the ink on Monday and it would still be good on Friday. I had to stop and add one solvent or the other every fifty balloons or so. Printing balloons was her job from then on. It kept her very busy.

In addition to selling printed balloons to customers in our store, we were also supplying wholesale balloon printing to party stores via a list of customers that came with the Sterling Rubber purchase. These were small retail stores like ours in and around the Chicago area. It was going so well we thought we'd try to expand our market. We got a mailing list of every party store in the country and sent flyers to all 1,400 of them. From that mailing we gained another fifty or so customers. Two years later I looked into getting another mailing list but the number of party stores had increased to over seven thousand. The writing was on the wall, but none of us saw it.

In addition to printing balloons, we were kept busy during those years with balloon launches. As soon as the warm weather came, it seemed every school in the area was renting a helium tank and buying balloons by the gross. Students would fill out cards with their name and address, attach them to a helium-filled balloon and send them on their way to see how far they would get. Most of them probably wound up in the Lake, but some made it across to dry land where someone would find the card and respond. It was a great geography lesson.

We did it at our family picnic, too. One of our cousins showed us a reply she'd received from someone who said he'd fished the card out of the River Thames in England. As we gathered around to look at the letter, there were grumblings about its authenticity. After all, a three-thousand mile trip for a balloon is hard to swallow. But someone spotting an index card attached to the remnants of a balloon in a river, taking time to fish it out, being able to read it, and then replying at his own expense staggers the imagination. She swore up and down that it was the real deal and finally said, "May God strike me dead if this is a fake." Of course, everyone scattered.

Adventures in Retail: The Dropped Ball

Once the word spread that we were printing balloons in house and in small quantities with fast service, people started expecting miracles. The biggest miracle we were ever asked for was from a distraught man who wanted ten thousand balloons printed by that afternoon. Now, the biggest order we'd ever done was for a local Ford dealer. It was for five thousand pieces and it took us almost three full workdays to complete. This man's order was out of the question.

I told him I could have done it if only he'd called us a week earlier. He tried everything. He offered to pay extra and help us get it done, but it was impossible and I told him that. We didn't even have that many balloons in stock. That's when he began to call me names and blame me for being unhelpful and uncooperative. He was going to alert the media and complain to the Better Business Bureau. Obviously, he'd dropped the ball and his ass was on the line. It was only after I told him I was going to call the police that he calmed down and left to face his fate. I'm just glad he wasn't carrying a weapon.

One Golden Weekend

March 21, 1987, marked the 50th anniversary of the day Jim Riley opened his store on Rhodes Avenue in Chicago. We had received some nice publicity for this milestone and had planned a small celebration in the store. I put a message on our marquee, attached some helium balloons on a string of pennants to the building, and ordered a cake, but we weren't expecting too much out of it. We were just looking forward to a normal busy Saturday.

We knew it was going to be special when the clowns arrived. Members of the Nairome Clown Troop had been our customers for years. We had supplied them with makeup, wigs, and accessories at a special clown discount and given their names to customers who were looking for clowns to perform at their parties. They returned the favor by showing up at our place between gigs. There were never fewer than two clowns in the store at any one time that day. They made balloon animals for the kids and entertained all who came in. When more showed up they went outside and waved at cars, directing them to our parking lot.

All through the day the store was filled with clowns, magicians, long-time customers, and former employees. The cake was gone before noon. We didn't make a whole lot of money but that was all right with us. We didn't want customers interfering with our fun anyway.

The following day we had a more formal celebration for the store's and my parents' anniversaries. Their anniversary was three weeks later but we figured we'd combine them. Two separate parties would have been way too expensive. Besides, claiming it was for the business's anniversary, we could write it all off.

The Chateau Bu-Sche at 115th and Cicero was one of our customers and they gave us a nice deal on one of their first-floor rooms. About 150 people showed up including relatives and friends, Magic Masters, current employees, and as many former employees as we could find.

We had a DJ but he didn't have much to do. Jim Wallace and Don Wiberg made speeches during dinner. Jim was very emotional when talking about how much my parents meant to him. Don took a more humorous approach. At one point he said he still had the first trick he'd ever bought at Riley's and that Dad still had the five dollar bill Don had spent for it. After dinner, Mom had everybody up doing skits that included masks and wigs from the store. It was all captured by a professional videographer.

The room was ours until 5:30 that afternoon but everyone was invited back to the store where the party continued into the night. Good thing my parents had that big space in their apartment, it was packed. Our kids were exhausted and we had to get them up for school the next day. We left around 9 but the party was in full swing and it ended late. It didn't matter how late it went. Dad was at the counter bright and early the next morning while the rest of us dragged ourselves in.

That weekend would be talked about for years. It made for lots of good memories, especially since it would be the last time my parents' long-time friends would all be together. They were in their 80s and their time was drawing short. Irene Keller, the store's first customer, passed away within a month of the party. That started a long string of wakes and funerals. Every time another one passed, Dad got out the anniversary video and watched it through misty eyes.

Eleanor and Jim in the store on their 50ᵗʰ Anniversary

Beverly Promotions

Shortly after the anniversary we were approached by the owners of Beverly Promotions, Jim and LaVerne Byerly. They sold advertising specialties, those small items that businesses give away to promote their goods and services. We had sent a lot of business their way when our customers asked us about printing services we didn't offer. In return, they supplied us with pencils with double erasers on them. When a customers were writing out headlines we'd hand them one of these pencils and watch as they flipped it two or three times before realizing it had no point. Then we'd give it to them because it had our name and information on it.

The Byerlys were looking to retire and wondered if we'd like to buy them out. It seemed like a good fit since we'd been sending them customers for years. They had a huge customer list and a salesman. Riley's was headed for the big time now. We agreed on a price of $16,000 and got into the advertising specialty business.

Their office in Palos Hills consisted of a few desks and a bunch of samples but mostly it was catalogs, hundreds of them. They filled several file cabinets. This was going to be a much bigger move than the balloon company so I rented a truck and took Chris George, our apprentice magician. I couldn't do much because it had been only six weeks since I'd injured my leg on the raft trip. Chris was invaluable. He was a skinny teenager but strong as an ox. He manhandled those filing cabinets like they were empty cardboard boxes.

It was there that I met our new salesman, Pete Potson. He was a character if there ever was one, and a salesman's salesman. He could take the shoes from your feet, sell them back to you for twice what you originally paid, and have you thanking him for the great deal. I'll never forget his first words to me. As he shook my hand he looked at my leg and said, "Jesus Christ! What the fuck happened to you?" I knew this was going to be a good relationship.

I was now an official advertising specialty counselor. There are hundreds of ad specialty suppliers, carrying tens of thousands of items from abacuses to zipper pullers, all custom-printed to the client's order. With Pete's help and a microfiche supplied by the Advertising Specialty Institute of Bucks County, Pennsylvania, I was able to quickly find anything a customer wanted. I even had a special office in the way back of the store where I could meet with clients away from the distractions of the main selling area. The walls were lined with samples and all the catalogs were within easy reach.

Pete's customers were the bigger accounts and he survived on the commissions. He did quite well for himself. The Teamsters union was one of the biggest, spending anywhere from five to ten thousand dollars at a time. They did that two or three times a year. They paid quickly but insisted that everything be American made. I can't tell you how many nights Pete and I sat in my office removing "Made in China" stickers from the thousands of keychains, flashlights, or gift baskets the Teamsters had purchased. We did what it took to keep a client happy.

I had originally kept Beverly Promotions as a separate business to avoid confusing their customers, but keeping two sets of books was a nightmare. So, as Beverly's customers came to know us, I incorporated Beverly Promotions into Riley's.

Because of Beverly Promotions we got our first fax machine. Since all orders had to be placed with suppliers out of state, we had to mail them, which could slow down the process by days. Sometimes we didn't have that luxury, especially if we needed a proof for the customer. That could take more than a week by mail, two weeks if we had to supply a signed proof back to the printer. Then production could begin. The fax allowed us to place orders the same day and get proofs back the following day. The internet later allowed us to send orders and artwork instantly, but the fax was state of the art in the late 80s.

Adventures in Retail: I'm Not a Fan

Pete's customers were Pete's but new advertising specialty customers who came through the door or called on the phone were mine. I sent him the bigger corporate customers and I mainly worked with people getting small quantities of items for personal use for weddings or birthdays, for example. One such order was for a girl who wanted hand fans printed for her Southern-style wedding in the northwest suburbs of Chicago.

These cardboard fans are shaped like palm leaves and printed with palm fronds on the edges. There is a blank area in the middle of both sides for imprinting. They're stapled to flat wooden sticks that look like they could be tongue depressors.

The first thing she asked me was what kind of wood the sticks were made of. I will not print the first thought that came to mind, or even the second. Maybe somebody had an allergy to balsa so I made a call and found out for her.

Once the sticks were deemed OK, she faxed me what she wanted printed on both sides, all standard fare and nothing to get excited about. She paid in full with a credit card and I placed the order. The wedding was three weeks away so there was no worry about any rush. Then the problems started.

She started calling in changes, nothing major like having to replace a bridesmaid or groomsman, just stupid nit-picky stuff. First, she wanted none of the backs printed, then half the backs, then three-quarters of the backs. Every day it was something new: a different font, this name larger, that name smaller, insert a nickname, take it out. With ten days to go, she called yet again and I told her I couldn't guarantee on-time delivery if there were any more changes. She called in three more changes after that. This was all for something that would most likely be tossed in the trash after the ceremony.

I stayed on top of this with the company and the order shipped UPS Second Day air on Wednesday, guaranteed to be there by Friday afternoon. She started calling Friday morning in full panic mode wondering where her fans were. There was no internet back then so tracking an order in real time was out of the question. By four p.m. she called in tears wondering what she was going to do if they didn't show up by her seven o'clock wedding. I reminded her that I had warned her about this if she kept making changes. I told her I had done all I could and it wasn't my fault if they were late. And she wasn't getting her money back.

The fans arrived by five as advertised and the wedding, and her life, weren't ruined. I wonder if she's still married.

Outside Activities

Dad ate, drank and slept the store. He thought about the store night and day. Any conversation I ever had with him eventually wound its way back to the store. He rarely said anything, but I know it bothered him that I didn't have the same fervor that he did for Riley's. One time he accused me of having too many outside activities, like this was some kind of monastery. I will not print his reaction to my injury after the raft trip.

As my leg began to heal, the doctor told me to do something aerobic to aid the process. I never was much of a runner and walking didn't interest me. Before our sons came along, Judy and I had spent a lot of Sunday mornings with the girls riding our bikes up and down the lakefront in Chicago. I used to take all the kids out after supper, too. But those rides were less than ten miles and the longest I'd ever gone was twenty miles. It was time to ramp that up.

I got up every morning and pedaled seven miles at first, increasing to twelve. The boys and I still went riding after supper.

Then I did a ride sponsored by a local bicycle club. Starting from a central location, riders are given maps and emergency numbers in case they get lost. They follow arrows spray-painted in the road that direct them on a ride of 50 or 100 kilometers, or 50 or 100 miles until they're back at the starting point. There are designated rest areas along the way where riders can have something to eat or refill their water bottles. The 100-miler, or century, is the bicycle equivalent of a marathon for runners. That was my goal.

That first year I did a couple of metric half centuries. That's 50 kilometers or 31 miles. They felt pretty good even with my injured leg. I completed a metric century or 62 miles before summer's end.

The next summer, 1988, I bought a Schwinn Tempo, a 12-speed triathlete's bike with skinny high-pressure tires. I rode every day, 15 miles before work, 25 miles or more on days off, and a metric century every time one of the local bike clubs had a ride. By August the metric centuries were getting easier. One ride from the College of DuPage in Glen Ellyn to Plainfield and back went more than 70 miles and was a piece of cake.

Sunday, September 11, 1988, was the Crank Country Century out of Valparaiso, Indiana. That was the day I was going to try a hundred miler. I picked this one because it was rated as relatively flat. I didn't want to tackle a hilly hundred on my first attempt.

I was so excited I woke up at 3 a.m. and couldn't go back to sleep. By 5 a.m. I was on the road. Two hours later I was signed in, had my map, emergency numbers, and two bottles of water. I was ready. My goal was to finish in eight hours. I did it in six and a half and made it home in time for cake as we were celebrating my Dad's and my son Ed's birthdays. I was in bed early that night.

I still have that Schwinn and still ride it as much as possible, just not a hundred miles at a time.

The following year, two of my bowling buddies, Bob O'Neill and Gordy Lakomy, who had already earned their amateur radio licenses, finally got me to go for mine. Not that they had to twist my arm much. Listening to the dots and dashes of Morse code and the voices from distant lands on my parents' monster radio in the apartment on Rhodes, and later on their Grundig Majestic on Aberdeen, I always knew I wanted to be a ham.

One Sunday afternoon in 1971 sealed the deal. My cousin on my mother's side, Ray Anderson, had just earned his license. As I watched him operate his rig that day, he asked if I wanted to try. Nervously, I spoke with a station in South America. I have no recollection of what we talked about but I was hooked.

Work dominated most of my time and I had a family to raise, so ham radio went on the back burner for eighteen years. Besides, the test was very technical and I wasn't sure I could pass it. Plus, I had other "outside activities" like beer can collecting and metal detecting to keep me busy.

By the spring of 1989 the beer can collection had long since been sold or sent off for recycling and metal detecting had lost its allure. Hamfesters Radio Club was holding classes for the novice license at Oak Forest High School. I signed up and passed the written test by the third week and the five word-per-minute Morse code test five weeks later. It seemed an eternity before my license came, but a month later I was licensed by the Federal Communications Commission as Amateur Radio Station KB9CYL.

In the ensuing years, I have upgraded my license to Amateur Extra, the top level, and served Hamfesters Radio Club as president for two terms, vice president for many more, board member for more than twenty years, and chairman of our Field Day committee since 1994. Field Day is an emergency exercise where we pretend commercial electrical power and telephone communications have been knocked out. We set up generators, antennas, and radio stations in an open field and make contacts with similar stations around the world. Globally, more than 30,000 people take part in this event. It's always the last full weekend in June.

Via my Amateur Radio license, I have become trained by the National Weather Service as a tornado spotter. That led me to join the Homer Glen Emergency Management Agency where I hold the rank of lieutenant. I have also taken part in a school's Amateur Radio contact with an American astronaut aboard the Russian MIR space station, operated from the radio room of the U-505 submarine at the Museum of Science and Industry in Chicago, and made contacts in Europe from the deck of the SS Badger car ferry in Lake Michigan.

I guess the monastic life just wouldn't be for me. I like my outside activities too much.

The Wheels Start Coming Off

By 1989 everything was running like a well-oiled machine. We had six full-time employees, two part-timers, and an outside salesman. The balloon machine was running almost constantly, turning out orders for our local customers and our party store clients around the country. Pete Potson was bringing in orders right and left. We were shipping orders every day for the catalog house that we were supplying. We were cranking out more than ten thousand headlines every year. We were on our way to our highest-grossing year ever.

Jim Wallace had been a signalman in the Navy in World War II and was helping me with my Morse code. I had upgraded my amateur radio license from novice to technician but felt like I was lying when I said I held a technician license. I am definitely not technical. I needed to increase my code speed from five words per minute to thirteen in order to upgrade to the general class. Morse code is like riding a bicycle. Once you learn it, you never forget it. He was helping me during rare slow times in the store, but he seemed somehow distracted.

Halloween that year was as busy as usual but everything changed on Monday, October 23. Jim wasn't at the door at his usual time and he didn't call in. That wasn't like him. When I got the chance, I called and found out from his wife, Marj, that he'd woken up disoriented and unable to keep his balance. We later learned that the diagnosis was brain cancer. That's why he'd seemed distracted. He knew something was wrong but didn't want to find out. When he did, it was too late. The cancer had spread and he died six weeks later.

Despite being a founding member of Magic Masters, Dad wasn't a great magician. He had a few tricks that he really liked and did well, but had no clue about the more technical items in Jim's magic department. He didn't do card magic at all because he liked to play poker and didn't want anyone to think he was cheating. Besides that, he'd just turned 80. Learning all these new tricks was out of the question. I had dabbled in magic as a kid but never got proficient in it.

So we decided to sell it all. Billy Bishop, a renowned magician from Vaudeville days, had opened a store in Berwyn and offered to take all we had. What none of us had realized was that Jim had been squirreling magic away in his storage area. Some shipping boxes were ten years old and had never been opened. A final inventory showed a lot more than we expected but Billy graciously stuck to his offer and took it all. And so the magic era ended at Riley's Trick Shop.

That was the biggest mistake we ever made. Magicians who hadn't heard about Jim were, of course, saddened at his passing but were more upset about the fact that we were out of the magic business. One, standing amid all the costumes, masks, wigs, hats, T-shirts, and over-the-hill gifts remarked, "So you've got nothing left to sell?" Magicians are remarkably focused on magic. When word got out that Riley's was going out of the magic business, the rumor mill had us going completely out of business.

Not long after Jim left us, Pete Potson passed away and we lost our promotional salesman. The advertising specialty business took a real nosedive because there was no way I could take his place. Running the store was tough enough. Going out on sales calls and three-hour, booze-filled lunches just weren't going to happen, tempting as the idea might be. We tried other salesmen. Some just didn't work out. Others learned the business from us, then set out on their own and became our competition.

To add insult to injury, some of our ad specialty suppliers decided they didn't want our "little" orders. We'd always met their minimums but that wasn't good enough for them. Our clients, especially those who bought calendars, would have had to double or triple their orders and they weren't ready to do that. So they just stopped ordering. It seems to me that a bunch of small orders is a good as one large order but big business doesn't see it that way.

The balloon business started to deflate, too. Environmentalists were making a big deal about how harmful balloons were. They seemed to forget that balloons are made of natural latex and are totally biodegradable. Schools, wanting to be politically correct, stopped having their springtime balloon launches.

Balloon printing took a hit, too. Those 7,000 party stores that had popped up got the notice of big business. Huge party mega-centers began appearing all across the country and the mom and pop party stores disappeared almost overnight. They were the bread and butter of our balloon printing business; the mega stores weren't interested.

While the expansion of the party store business affected our Halloween a little, it devastated our New Year's Eve. The week between Christmas and New Year's Eve had been a boom time. The middle of our sales area was piled with boxes of hats, horns, noisemakers, serpentine streamers, and blowouts. On a row of tables was open stock so those having smaller gatherings could get exactly what they needed. Jim Wallace, who loved working with his hands, filled bags with dozen quantities of everything. Three or four times a day the store would be filled with the sound of another box of 100 metal noisemakers being dumped into open stock. With party stores on just about every corner, and liquor stores, grocery stores, and drug stores selling New Year's Eve party favors, there was no reason for anyone to come to us. The week after Christmas used to be one of the busiest weeks of the year. It became a time to close and take a vacation.

Yes, the wheels started coming off but we still had enough wheels to run on and there was plenty of road ahead. That road would be more crowded but we'd be riding in a smaller vehicle, more nimble and able to change direction. The businesses we'd acquired in the 80s would take a back seat to our core activities.

The Family Grows

The 90s had begun on a difficult note but it wasn't all doom and gloom. All four of our kids had worked for us at different times, usually on

Saturdays when we all rode in together. My wife, Judy, had been working in the catalog department at Penney's in Orland Square for a few years. With Jim gone and Dad slowing down, I needed someone to take up the slack. Judy started for us in 1991. She kept her job at Penney's for a while but two jobs were too much for her and she started full-time for us shortly after.

Is it possible to work with your spouse and maintain a civil relationship? It's difficult and I'm sure there were times when we both regretted the decision, Judy more so than me. But we had to see each other across the supper table after work and we did the best we could. Fortunately, the building was big enough that we could get away from each other when necessary and still do our jobs. The most important part of working with your spouse is to establish just who's boss. She let me think I was in charge and it worked out well for both of us.

The best way to handle working with each other and stay out of each other's way is to divide the duties. She took care of ordering, stocking, and displaying merchandise. I was in charge of the printing side and all the paperwork. Of course, we both took care of customers.

After our daughter, Colleen, got out of St. Joseph's College in 1993 she came to work for us, too. Now it really was becoming a family business as a fourth generation came on full-time.

Shortly after starting with us, Colleen married Roger Jage, a police officer in Western Springs, Illinois. Three years later they presented us with our first grandchild, Courtney.

Kristen married Al Gioia, an electrician, shortly after Courtney was born. Kristen didn't want to be married in our church because it didn't have a traditional aisle. So she had her wedding in an old church in the city. The church had an aisle, all right, but it didn't have air conditioning and the temperature that day was in the upper 90s with humidity to match. Fortunately, we worked in a novelty shop. We raided our shelves and provided every member of the bridal party with a battery-powered handheld fan. Our first grandson, Ethan, was born to them a few years later.

Evolution of T-shirt Printing: Computers

The shirt business kept us very busy. Where else could a customer order a single shirt printed to his or her order and walk out with it in a few minutes? Okay, it was more than a few minutes because we still had to go into the darkroom, do a setup one letter at a time on the Linographics machine and bring it up to run in the X-pres machine. Yes, it was a slow process but it was our only option and it worked very well.

In the early 90s we were contacted by a company called Vital Lasertype who sold a MacIntosh computer programmed for the printing business. It revolutionized our T-shirt printing. It offered thousands of scalable fonts and the customer could watch us do the setup, making corrections as we went. If a darkroom setup wasn't exactly what the customer wanted, we had to go back and start over. This new technology cut our production time drastically. It printed in black only and we could change colors in the X-pres machine, but we could still print only one color at a time. Even so, the Mac was a vast improvement.

About this time, customers started asking about photo shirts. The only way to get them done at that time was to send away and wait a couple of weeks. Since the last minute is the only motivator for most people, waiting weeks just didn't cut it. We invested in a color copier. All this copier did was copy; no enlargements, no reductions, no adjustments of any kind. And, most importantly, it offered no reversals. A T-shirt transfer must be printed in reverse or else the image is backward when printed on the shirt. We overcame that by making one copy on a transparency and placing it backward on the copier plate and copying it again. This copy came out backward on the transfer paper and printed correctly on the shirt. Of course, multiple copies degrade the original and the picture terrible on the shirts. But at least the customers had photos on and they were happy.

It wasn't long before color copying technology improved and we full-sized Canon color copier that enlarged, reduced, and reversed images transferring. It was great for photo shirts and other graphics that customer brought in, but we still couldn't print setups in color.

That changed when our Mac stopped working. Since we had already sold the Linographics machine, we were unable to produce any custom T-shirt, cap, or button orders. Of course, we were in a state of panic. We still had plenty of commercial transfers to choose from but we were completely unable to design anything special for our customers.

Re-enter the X-pres Corporation. They had changed their name to Spectra and introduced a whole new system: a PC connected to a subli-mation printer. Bundled in was CorelDraw 3, a graphics program with hundreds of fonts and thousands of graphics that could all be scaled and manipulated any way we wanted in as many colors as necessary. The sub-limation printer had a ribbon that had strips of red, green, and blue. As it passed over the transfer paper it thermally deposited ink from the ribbon in quantities determined by the image on the screen. It took almost three minutes to complete a single transfer. It was a very wasteful process as only the parts of the ribbon necessary to print the file were used. The rest of the ribbon went on the take-up reel and was thrown out. Still, it was the state of the T-shirt printer's art.

We still used the color copier for photo shirts and button setups.

Adventures In Retail: Go Bears

We put that new printing setup to good use almost immediately. On a Tuesday morning a distraught customer came in bemoaning the fact that he'd lost a bet on the previous night's game. He had foolishly bet on the Bears. More

over the Packers. The ultimate foolishness
Packers on Monday Night Football. The
Monday nights and the Packers did. The
'l and this was a sucker bet if there ever

...ne loser would wear the other team's hat to work for
...1f I could help him. I told him there wasn't much I could do
...betting but I sure had an idea for the hat.

On the computer I designed a logo that approximated, not copied (in case anyone from the NFL, or their lawyers, is reading), the Packers's design in gold and green. Arched above, it read **GREEN BAY** in green letters. Below, it read **PACKERS** in green with the **A** changed to an **E**. I printed that on the front of a gold trucker's hat.

He walked out happily wearing his "new favorite hat," but I don't know if he got away with it with his friends at work. He never came back. I was happy to have struck one small blow for my team.

On The Road Again

It was getting more difficult for us to travel since all the changes had come to the store. With Jim Wallace gone and Dad's mind deteriorating it was hard to get away in the early 90s. Besides, with Judy working with me that meant two of us would be gone at the same time. We spent most of our vacation time taking day trips around the local area or just hanging around our backyard pool.

Mom and Dad, however, traveled extensively. There were no more trips to exotic, far-flung locales for them. Instead they did more "mystery trips" and other package vacations with the friends they'd made on previous trips. Of course, they had a ball wherever they went. They gambled on a Mississippi River boat, went to Disney World and San Antonio, among others. In '93 they were in South Carolina when the so-called "storm of the century" hit. This

huge nor'easter dumped tons of snow up north, caused massive f
they were, and extended their stay because flights weren't getting o

Jim & Eleanor all dressed up for another mystery tour.

On a trip to King's Island in Ohio, Mom had a bad fall and horribly mangled her right arm. Gamely, she just iced it and stayed with the trip. When she got home, her entire upper arm was swollen and black from her elbow to her shoulder. Fortunately, nothing was broken and the doctor gave her some therapy to do. She was told to do ten repetitions of different exercises each day. As a self-described "tough old Swede" she did twenty reps three times a day. It *oods where*

...

...tely heal but the doctor said he'd never seen ...'n their fifties. Mom was 82.

...rried, our house was inundated with fly- ...place. It was our 25th anniversary and ...for a few days. We picked Forrest Hills in

...there, Judy wanted to turn back. Each room was a private ...looked, on the outside at least, to be nothing more than a shack. ...e inside was quite different. In addition to the fireplace, living room, and dining area, it had a canopy bed with a hot tub next to it. We stayed.

Breakfast and supper were included in the package and served in a communal dining room on candle-lit tables for two. It was a honeymoon resort, after all. The food was home-cooked and excellent. The most striking thing for me was how quiet the meals were. The room was full but all the conversations were in hushed tones. And no, we weren't the only non-honeymooners there. Another couple was celebrating their 50th anniversary.

Two years later, the kids sent us to Disney World. It was the first time Judy and I had ever flown together. Disney World without having children along is the only way to go. There's no worry about anybody getting lost and there's no fighting or crying. We liked it so much we took our friends, Bob and Sandy Langland, the next year.

Adventures in Retail: Whiskey Tango Foxtrot

Most of our adventures in retail revolve around the printing business because of all the variables involved. There was the guy who kept bringing in black shirts to be printed even though I told him over and over that our process didn't work on dark colors. Every time he came in I had to go through the same explanations again and again and he'd ask, "What about this or that color print."

By this time I'd had it because he'd get me upset just by walking in the door. I pulled myself up to my full five foot eight and yelled, "There is no color that will work on black. None. Zip. Zero. Nada."

He considered this for a moment and asked, "What about yellow?"

"When did yellow stop being a color?" I replied and walked away. He eventually left and never came back.

Then there was the woman who wanted polo shirts for a family barbecue. It was an easy job, ash gray polo shirts with the design printed on the pocket. She approved the artwork, I ordered the shirts, and did the printing.

When she came to pick them up, she was appalled at how "shitty" they looked and started ranting. Now, I am my harshest critic and nothing ever got to the customer unless it passed my inspection. These shirts were perfect. She started showing them to customers in the store and they thought they were perfect, too. Still, she wasn't happy and wanted them redone. There was nothing I could do to improve them but they were marked up enough that another run wouldn't hurt us that much. Besides, sometimes you can do the exact same thing a second time and the customer will happy with it. Go figure.

I called my supplier to reorder but they were out. My other suppliers were out, too. Apparently, the mill was behind and these particular shirts were unavailable anywhere. After I called to explain this to her, she called every T-shirt supplier in town to bitch at them and then she called the mill to let them have it, too.

She came back in to get the shirts as they were but didn't want to pay for them, probably her goal all along. After a long shouting match, we finally agreed on a discounted price but she still wasn't happy. I decided to leave before I killed her. She told my daughter that I should learn to relax.

I said afterward that I would love to find her with her car broken down on some desolate stretch of road. I'd tell her that I'd love to help but she wouldn't be satisfied with my work. See ya!

I found out later that her family barbecue was in the path of a hurricane that hit shortly after she arrived. You gotta love karma.

Another woman wanted a left chest print on a plain T-shirt. She was very particular and wanted to make sure I knew exactly where she wanted it. I laid out a shirt for her, made a paper proof of the design, and she placed it on the shirt. I had no problem with customers doing this because they should get their print exactly where they want it…within reason. The problem was that her placement put half the print in the armpit and I couldn't convince her otherwise. She showed it to other customers and they all said the same thing, it was too close to the armpit. Finally, she agreed that I was right and was very happy with the finished product. Her parting words were, "Thanks for making me miss my lunch hour."

It was no consolation to her that I'd missed mine, too.

The Final Word

With the age of electronics upon us, the landscape of the trick and joke business shifted. The only new joke items coming out were of the shocking variety. Where there had once been just the shock book, now there were shocking pens, lighters, and pop cans.

Out of nowhere came an item that took the country by storm. It was a keychain attached to a little box about the size of a car's remote. Push the button and it swore. It was sold under many names but our supplier called it The Final Word. It randomly played four sayings better saved for a locker room or military barracks. We couldn't keep it in stock. Most orders were spoken for before they came in and, at one point, we had almost two hundred people on a waiting list.

At that time, our supplier was out of stock but he directed us to someone on the north side who might be able to help. I called and he told me he had plenty but didn't want to drive all the way to Worth from Rogers Park. I didn't want to drive all the way to Rogers Park so we agreed to meet at a place we both knew well, the rock 'n roll McDonald's in downtown Chicago. We met in the parking lot at ten that evening. I paid him in cash. He unloaded bags of Final Words from his trunk and put them in mine.

I know this story doesn't sound exciting but I found out later that our meeting place had been under surveillance by Chicago Police and the DEA for drug dealing. Imagine how shady it must have looked: two cars, one with out-of-state license plates, backed up trunk to trunk, one driver exchanging a lot of cash for plastic bags of who knew what. Imagine further if my car had been pulled over after the exchange with the cop examining the bags in my trunk and one of them telling him to do something anatomically impossible to himself.

Fortunately, that didn't happen, and the Final Word, like most other fads, ran its course.

Fun Facts

Just about everyone has heard about whoopee cushions, joy buzzers, and other joke items but very few know how they came about or how they evolved. Here is the story, thanks to all the good folks who contribute articles to Wikipedia.

Most of the novelties we have today are the work of Soren Adam Sorenson. Soren emigrated from Denmark in 1873. While working for a dye company in 1904 he found that one of the products he sold caused people to sneeze. He isolated the irritating ingredient and formed the Cachoo Sneezing Powder Company in Plainfield, New Jersey, when orders started piling up. When that craze faded, he set out to create new products. It was about this time he changed the name of the company to SS Adams.

In 1915, in response to his wife's nagging about a stuck jam jar, he invented the precursor to the snake nut can. Called the Snake Jam Jar, it contained a fabric-wrapped spring that jumped out when the top was opened. That evolved into the Snake Nut Can, the Snake Mint Can, and the larger Snake Peanut Brittle Can which originally had three six-foot cloth-covered snakes. Today the springs are covered in plastic and there are only two snakes in the Peanut Brittle Can. Soren's grandson invented the Snake Potato Chip can in 1995.

Another Adams invention was the Joy Buzzer which he patented in 1932. Wound up on a spring and worn like ring, it buzzes the victim's hand when he shakes hands with the wearer. Contrary to popular belief, it does not give an electric shock. The success of this device allowed Sorenson to move to a bigger building and greatly expand his company. Except for a few minor modifications, the Joy Buzzer is still the same design today.

One item Sorenson almost missed out on was the Whoopee Cushion. Invented by workers at the Jem Rubber Company of Toronto, Canada, who were experimenting with scrap pieces of rubber, it's been a standby of the joke industry since the 1930s. Sorenson turned it down as "too vulgar" so Jem Rubber sold it to the Johnson Smith Company. Sorenson reconsidered when he saw how successful it was for Johnson Smith and quickly came out with his own version, the Raspberry Cushion.

It's still sold in its original version which has to be inflated after each use, but in the early 90s they tried a self-inflating Whoopee Cushion. It had limited success and was quickly replaced with the remote control whoopee cushion, also called the Fart Machine, not an Adams product. In that version, a receiver is hidden behind some furniture or under a table and is controlled by a handheld transmitter. It plays farting sounds from a short toot to a long blast from as far as 100 feet away.

One of our customers told us he was taking it to a wake of a notorious gas-passer. He was going to place it behind the casket and hit the transmitter whenever anyone approached. Whether he did it or not we don't know, but that's one wake I would have enjoyed going to.

Over the years Sorenson claimed to have developed over six hundred items and received patents on forty of them. Among his inventions are the bug in the ice cube, dribble glass, itching powder, stink bomb, and the squirt nickel. Sorenson died in 1963 at the age of 84.

Fox Thing in the Morning

In the spring of 1997 we sent out press releases about Riley's upcoming 60th anniversary. We got the usual responses from the local newspapers but I was surprised to get a call from a producer at the Fox station in Chicago, Channel 32. She asked if I would be interested in doing a live remote from our store on April Fool's Day. I'd be talking to Bob Sirott on Fox Thing in the Morning. She didn't have to ask me twice.

Bob Sirott had been the morning host of First Thing in the Morning on NBC 5 in Chicago. When they abruptly fired him in 1993 he went to Fox and started Fox Thing in the Morning, probably as a rebuke to his former employer. He shared the anchor desk with Marianne Murciano who would later become his wife. The show was the standard morning fare: news, weather, sports, and features. In one of those features they sent a crew to a business, school, or government office to interview someone there. Some interviewees did quite well, others not so much. I hoped I'd be in the former category.

The day before the big event I got a call from WGN Morning News. They wanted me to come to their studio with some April Fool's Day items for a live segment on their show. I told them I was already booked but if they could pick me up and return me in their news chopper I'd be glad to do it after I was finished with Fox. They never got back to me.

I stayed late that evening, making sure all the shelves were fully-stocked, or at least fully-faced, not an easy task the night before April Fool's Day. The shelves are usually depleted by then.

I was out of bed at 5 a.m. on the big day. The Fox truck with its telescoping antenna was visible up and down 111th Street when I arrived at 6:30. The crew consisted of a producer, the camera man, and an engineer in the truck. Our segment was to air at 7:30 and there was a lot to do to get ready. They were all ready. It was me they needed to work on. To one side of my belt they hooked a receiver with an ear plug. To the other side they hooked a transmitter connected to a small microphone on my collar. After the sound checks, there was nothing to do but wait with these heavy objects attached to me. No wonder news people get paid so much.

About five minutes before we went on the air, my earpiece came alive and I found out why some people had had problems with their interviews. The sound was very tinny and, when Bob and Marianne both talked at the same time, it was terribly garbled. Fortunately, my amateur radio experience of digging voices out of static and other atmospheric noise was a big help as I was able to make out everything they said.

Since it was April Fool's Day I set up a prank with the producer and engineer who cleared it with the people back at the station. When it was my turn to speak I just mouthed, "Hi, Bob. Hi, Marianne," without saying anything. There was no monitor to look at, just the camera, so I couldn't see it until later when I got to look at the tape, but their jaws just dropped. Then I came back with a cheery "April Fool." Bob knew he'd been had. He just shook his head and the interview began. We talked about the history of Riley's, and some of the more popular tricks and jokes. As we went to commercial I flashed one of our headlines that said

RILEY'S TRICK SHOP
WELCOMES
FOX THING IN THE MORNING

It must have gone over very well because there were people at our door even as we were on the air. The producer had to keep them outside. We couldn't lock the door because of the cables leading from the camera to the truck.

It was all over in five minutes. I was freed from the electronics attached to me but the crew stayed another hour sending live shots of our customers back to the studio as the show went to commercial breaks. We took care of the early-bird customers and headed out to breakfast. The segment must have worked. We were busy the entire day.

Evolution of T-shirt Printing: Integration

As the lease expired on our color copier, it was time to look for something better. Something better came along in the form of a Ricoh color copier that hooked directly into our computer. Not only was it a copier, it was a printer and scanner too. What that meant for us was that we could scan a photo into our computer, make necessary adjustments, add text, and send it right back to the printer to make a T-shirt transfer. This machine could print three full-color pages a minute instead of the three minutes per page that the sublimation machine did. And we wouldn't be wasting all that sublimation ribbon. All would be wonderful.

At least that's what the salesman had said. When the scanner didn't work, he told me it was not compatible with our computer even though I had showed him what we were using. I had asked him repeatedly if our transfer paper would work with the Ricoh. He assured me it would. When the tech came to repair the machine the on its second day of operation, he told me it was never designed to work with transfer paper. I learned right then and there to never trust anyone, especially a salesman, who prefaces every answer with the words, "in a sense."

Fortunately, I had the foresight to purchase a bumper-to-bumper warrantee with the lease. My experience with the color copier taught me that. A fuser roller assembly which seals the print onto the paper was more than $1,000 to replace. Transfer paper has a coating that transfers with the print to hold it on the shirt. Fuser rollers hate transfer paper, so we sure got our money's worth out of that warrantee. And we got to know all the repair guys during the next four years. We called them at least once a week.

Since the color copier had a propensity to crash on a Friday evening and there was no tech support until Monday, we bought an ink-jet printer. That allowed us to use the less-desirable inkjet paper and stay in the T-shirt business on busy Saturdays.

When the copier was working, it was wonderful. Not only could we print three T-shirt transfers a minute but we could print hundreds of full-color button setups with graphics and photos.

For the next twelve years this was the state of the shirt printing art. After the Ricoh we went through two Minoltas. The Minolta machines were a little more robust but fuser rollers were still a problem. That allowed us to get to know a whole new bunch of service reps.

STOP THE PRESSES!!

Shortly after we got the new setup for T-shirts working, our computer headline printer abruptly stopped working. One morning we turned it on and put the big floppy disk in but nothing happened. Another try brought the same result. Not to worry, we'll just load the backup disk. Nothing. It wasn't long before calm problem-solving turned into full-scale panic. The company we'd bought the system from twelve years before was long gone. Nobody worked on 8086 computers anymore and we couldn't buy new software on 5.25-inch floppy disks. The computer world had passed this machine by.

For the first time in almost forty years, Riley's wasn't printing newspaper headlines. It really hurt to tell our customers that, especially those who had been getting headlines for every family event since Harry Truman was President. People looked forward to seeing their name in print for birthdays and anniversaries. What was I going to do with the thousands of headline blanks stored in the back of the building?

Finally, I resigned myself to the fact that we were out of the headline business for good. Then, sitting in church one Sunday, I had a revelation, a real "DUH" moment. The answer was right in front of me. Why couldn't our new T-shirt setup work for headlines?

The printer could handle that size paper with no problem but would it accept sheets that were folded? Headline blanks going through the old machine were 15 inches wide and 22 inches high. We'd have to remove the pin-feeder strips and fold each sheet to 15 by 11 to get it in the color printer. The first attempt failed miserably as the paper jammed in the first set of rollers. I had to fool it into thinking it was taking a single sheet. A small piece of tape holding the leading edge together did the trick.

All that was left to do was set up a headline template in the T-shirt computer. Now we were back in the headline business with the bonus of being able to add photos and color print. All we had to do was remove miles of pin-feeder strips from all the sheets, and tape the leading edges of each and every sheet before sending it through the printer. If there was a market for evenly-spaced holes on half-inch wide strips of paper, we would have had that market cornered.

When the pin-fed papers finally ran out, we ordered a whole new batch of headline sheets. They came without pin-feeders, of course, and each sheet was folded in half like the old proof press sheets. When we moved out of Chicago we changed the name of the paper from The Chicago Page to a more generic The News Gazette. Our new sheets left that area blank so we could put in the name of any newspaper the customer wanted. The only stipulation is that they couldn't use the name of a real paper. The major newspapers all have lawyers. We didn't.

This setup served us very well until the lease on the Ricoh expired. When we switched to Minolta copiers we found that they didn't like the headlines no matter how much tape we put on them. So it was time to scramble again. Fortunately, most of the inkjet manufacturers make printers with wide carriages that will handle headline paper. No need to tape, either.

Headline printing is hard on ink jet printers. That's especially true of those that feed paper from the bottom. It has to go under the print area and wrap around the back. After a while the paper starts binding up and does terrible things to the print heads. We went through two HP's before settling on an Epson 1400. It feeds from the back, sending the paper through in a straight line.

I bet Dad never could have imagined where headline printing would go when he bought the original proof press way back in 1949.

BUTTON, BUTTON, WHO'S GOT THE BUTTON?

That was always the question when we ran out of button parts. Originally it was N.G. Slater from New York, but we needed a local supplier. We eventually found a company called Promocraft, in Oak Park. They were close enough that we were able to get a box of parts delivered overnight via UPS, and they were a straight shot down Harlem Avenue if we couldn't wait that long.

In the summer of 1997 the owner, Al Wisawady, called to tell us he was getting rid of the button aspect of his business and asked if we'd like to buy it. Promocraft was also in advertising specialty business which he could run out of his home. Since we were already making buttons, this seemed like a good fit. The price was right, $16,000 for five hand-operated machines, five hydraulic machines, and 175 new customers.

We'd be adding 1.25-, 1.75-, and 3.5-inch buttons to the 2.25- and 3-inch buttons we already sold and we'd be buying parts directly from the manufacturer. That would cut our costs down. As an added bonus, we'd be able to cut up to fifty buttons at a time with our new cutter, as opposed to the old way of cutting buttons one at a time.

Cutting buttons requires cutting a circle of paper with the print on it to exactly the right diameter for the job. Cut it too big and it won't fit into the dye, too small and the button falls apart. The job can't be done with scissors because the insert has to be perfectly round. For years we used a cutter with a rotary blade wheel that cut a perfect circle by laying it over the print and forcing it down on the paper. The operator pushed down on a spherical handle and makes a circular motion. This was fine for short jobs but bigger jobs would do horrible things to the operator's palm. Bicycle gloves were needed to take care of that. Six cuts a minute was a good rate for this method.

The cutter that came with our new acquisition forces a circular blade down on the paper using six thousand pounds of force provided by a bottle jack, the same as one used to raise a car to change a tire. As long as the prints line up in the same place on each sheet, the operator can make a hundred or more cuts a minute. Fortunately, most color copiers and inkjet printers offer consistent placement of each print.

Once the prints were cut into circles, they were fed into our new hydraulic button machines. They worked pretty much the same way as the hand-operated machines with the exception that, instead of pulling a handle up and down by hand, an electric foot switch caused the dies to clamp together and release. That freed the operator's hands for inserting and removing the components used to make the buttons. Two hundred completed buttons an hour was a good rate.

Of all the customers that came with our new acquisition, we came to know Amos Harris of the Alabama Button Company in Montgomery the best. When he called to place an order I knew I'd be on the phone for half an hour or more. His stories of his Korean War days and time as a Chicago policeman were fascinating. He laughingly claimed to be one of only three black Republicans in the entire state of Alabama.

When he came back to Chicago on a visit, we met in person for the first time after more than ten years of talking on the phone. As his friend who'd come along was taking a picture of us together, Amos asked if it would be in color. I looked at the two of us and said that it would be in black and white. They could probably hear him laughing all the way down 111th Street.

There's no telling how many buttons we made over the years, but our acquisition of Promocraft probably propelled that number well into the hundreds of thousands.

www.HelloWorld

In the fall of 1999 we put our first website online. I had seen the marketing potential of the internet since I'd first heard of it but didn't know how to go about it. My daughter Colleen bought me a book that claimed it could help anyone build a website and publish it in twenty-four hours. It took longer than that even though no HTML (Hyper Text Markup Language, the lingo of the internet) was required, but we had a website published for Halloween of that year.

It wasn't much of a site, there was no e-commerce and some really bad pictures, but it did very well. That was probably because it was the only Halloween website out there. Customers had to place their orders via email or on the phone. Their credit cards had to be processed by entering their information by hand into our terminal. Sometimes numbers were transposed and we had to call them back to get the card number again. Then everything had to be packed up for shipping via UPS. We were running twenty to thirty orders a day this way. It doesn't sound like much but we still had a robust business over the counter and we had to do all this when time permitted. Many nights I was there until midnight packing orders. After a few hours' sleep I was back in early to get a jump on the overnight orders.

There were some pretty desperate people out there. On more than one Friday afternoon I was called by someone who needed a particular costume for a party the following night. UPS Saturday overnight delivery to a residence isn't cheap, but they wanted their costume and price was no object. A thirty-dollar costume delivered that way could result in fifty to sixty dollars in shipping charges. They were happy to pay it.

That worked fine for a couple of years, but the rest of the Halloween world was catching up and they were doing it with flashy websites, e-commerce, and PayPal. I had no clue how to do this and our website languished.

Three years later I was approached by Scott Sedwick of Hyperformance Media who offered to build us a website to rival anything our competitors did. He was true to his word.

It took many nights of shooting pictures and gathering information on my part. I built a small studio in the back of the store for shooting pictures of just about everything we had. Then he did his magic. In a very short time we had a seven hundred-item website where customers could pay via credit card or PayPal. All we had to do was print a packing list, get the item, and pack it up. That cut our processing time by ten to fifteen minutes per order. There were no problems with credit card numbers being transposed or bogus. That was all taken care of before the order got to us. It was a beautiful thing and it worked great for the next four years.

Scott made one big mistake: he taught me how to do the grunt work myself. I had to pay him each time I needed to add a new item to the site or edit an existing one. It was getting expensive just to maintain the thing. Since I'd programmed computers back in the 60s I thought I could do the maintenance myself. The basic structure was there, I just needed to learn how to adjust it. I didn't need to know HTML but I did have to learn the proper formatting and sizing for my pictures and how to use FTP (File Transfer Protocol) to get the entire website published. Through my many phone calls and several drives to his office in Schaumburg, Scott patiently worked me through it.

I got so good at it I could add an item, including shooting and processing the picture, in less than fifteen minutes. This was great because we couldn't afford to pay for having all the items added that we wanted to add. Over the next few years I built the website up to almost 1,500 unique items. Now we were on our way to a true internet presence. Our website was like our store with categories like Tricks, Hats, Wigs, Costumes, Makeup, Magic, Over the Hill Gifts, and more. It worked great until there was a problem with PayPal.

Due to the ton of spam I was receiving daily, I had to change my email address with PayPal. It sounded easy enough so I figured I'd do it myself. That was <u>my</u> big mistake. For some reason, the new email didn't work. The website was still working but our e-commerce wasn't. Payments were vanishing into cyberspace. Changing back to the old email didn't work either. Phone calls and emails to PayPal didn't resolve anything so I went crawling back to Scott. Phone calls and emails to him went unanswered. It was like he'd fallen off the face of the earth.

For Halloween 2006 I had to revert to the old way of taking internet orders but with a new twist. When an order came in, I had to phone the customers and ask them to cancel the order via PayPal. Then they had to give me their credit card information over the phone and I had to process it by hand.

That forced me to start working on the next version of Riley's website. Yahoo had a great small business package that provided website building tools and e-commerce all in one package. It wasn't as flashy as the site Scott built but it was very functional. Instead of nine pictures to a page, every category had thumbnail pictures of each item. A customer could click on the thumbnail for a larger picture and all the information on that item.

Fortunately, I could use the pictures from the old website. All I had to do was reenter all the product information. It took a few months but we were back on the web with a new website I was very proud of. I promised never to change my email address ever again.

You Will Not Be Forgotten

In the late summer of 2001, Judy's younger sister, Shirley, was turning fifty. She wanted to do something special with Judy and their older sister, Geri. After much deliberation they settled on a trip to Las Vegas. It was the first time the three of them had traveled together since they'd taken trips with their parents, and the first time they'd flown together. I drove Geri, Judy, and Shirley to Midway Airport on a clear, bright Tuesday morning in September. They were as excited as schoolgirls.

It was an 8 a.m. flight so I had to get them there by 6. It was too early to go to the store and too late to go back to bed so I decided to go back home and work on my mountain bike. A bunch of us were planning to ride the Sugar River bike trail in Wisconsin later in the month and I needed to replace my rear wheel. Off-road cycling takes a heavy toll on aluminum rims. Mine was bent beyond repair.

Our garage is right off the family room so I left the door open and listened to the WGN morning news on Channel 9 as I worked. I had mounted the tire on the new wheel and was just putting it on the bike when the flash came that a plane had crashed into the north tower of the World Trade Center in New York. I dropped what I was doing and went in to watch. Like everyone else around the world I knew it wasn't an accident as I watched the second plane hit the south tower.

The girls' plane was allowed to take off before the order came to get all flights on the ground. Now the concern was what would happen to their flight. As I drove to work down Southwest Highway from 131st to 111th I could see Sears Tower in the distance and wondered if it would be attacked, too.

When I got to the store I tried calling the airline but was told any information about flights was classified as a matter of national security. National security? Gimme a break! I didn't care about their national security. I just wanted to know that my wife was safe. When Colleen came in, she started calling airports directly to see if her mother's flight had landed there. Finally, after tearful pleading with someone at the regional airport in Peoria, Illinois, she found that they were safely on the ground.

Judy told me later that the plane's captain had originally told them that they had to return to Chicago from their location somewhere over Iowa. A few minutes later he said he had to put the plane down NOW. They were never told about the attacks and thought something was wrong with the plane. Only when they landed did they find out what happened, and that was from a TV in the airport. It took at least an hour after they landed but Judy was finally able to get through and let me know she was all right.

There was nothing going on at the store that day. We took in a whole $2.50 in two hours. My concerns for the future of Riley's and the upcoming Halloween season were put on the back burner as I had to get my wife and her sisters back home.

Peoria is only two and a half hours from home and the trip was uneventful. I found the girls without difficulty. They were anxious to get home. As we drove east on I-74 I noticed a contrail very high in the sky to my left. The no-fly order was in effect so this gave me pause. Then I saw a larger contrail and several smaller ones around it. This could mean only one thing: I was seeing Air Force One as it headed back to Washington.

Judy and I had the next day off, but the store was open. People were still in shock and nothing was going on. Bored, one of the part-time high school kids went outside to the curb and waved one of our American flags. That almost caused a traffic accident as people whipped off 111th Street into our parking lot to see if we had any flags. The next day we sold out every flag we had. From our largest outdoor flags to our smallest hand-held flags to flag lapel pins, they all went. Thursday we ordered every flag we could get out hands on from our local suppliers. They were sold out by the weekend. We couldn't fly any more in because of the no-fly rule. Besides, every formerly unsold flag in the country was now adorning someone's car, front porch, or yard.

Then people discovered that we print T-shirts. Most brought in their own designs. Some were classy like the image of the twin towers and the words "You Will Not Be Forgotten." Others condemned terrorists and terrorism with words best not printed here. It was good to know the First Amendment was still in force. We were working overtime as orders kept piling in. While the income was nice, deep down inside I didn't want to profit too much from a tragedy like 9/11. We lowered the price of shirts relating to 9/11 and donated some of the profits to the Salvation Army. When it was all over we'd sent them more than $5,000.

Everything had settled down by the end of September and I took that bike trip with my friends. I'd been too busy to do any riding since September 11th and, as I headed out, I discovered that my bike was just as I'd left in that morning when the news came out. The rear wheel wasn't tightened and the chain not attached. In my excitement to hit the trail I didn't notice. I didn't get far. Fortunately, I had my trusty tool kit with me and a quick trailside repair set that right.

Geri, Shirley, and Judy have never flown together again.

Our family did, though. Way before September 11 we'd booked a trip that we were not about to miss. Two months after that tragic day, Judy, our son Jim, our daughter Kristen and her husband Al, and I boarded an Aer

Lingus Airbus 330 and headed northeast to Ireland. We'd rented a cottage overlooking Galway Bay and toured the country by car and train.

How else would the founder of Riley's Trick Shop dress for his 90th birthday?

The Changing of the Guard

Sometime during the late 90s Dad finally retired. His body didn't let him down but his brain did. This man who could total an invoice in his head and determine a price for an individual item instantly just by looking at the dozen price was unable to do even the simplest addition or subtraction. Remembering an item number for even a few seconds was lost to him. He had no clue that that number correlated to a location in the store even though it was he who set up the store's numbering system.

Our Halloween merchandise was located in drawers running the length of the building in an aisle behind the main counters. Dad was constantly complaining that it was getting too hard for him to walk all the way to the back of the store a hundred times a day to fill orders. His solution was to move everything up front. I tried to explain to him that the front was full of merchandise already and there was no room, but he kept telling me we had to do it. It was obvious he was getting frustrated.

It wasn't his decreasing mental capacity that made him quit, nor was it the long walk to the back of the store. It was a simple argument.

We had just received an order of temporary tattoos, designs that transfer from backing paper to your skin. He was reading the label and mentioned that it said they were washable. "Oh, they wash right off," he said.

"No," we told him, "that means you can wash your skin and they won't come off."

"Ahhhh, you're nuts. It washes off, definitely." When he said "definitely" the argument was over, definitely.

I explained it to him, as did Judy and Colleen. He didn't budge. As with the store-closing controversy on Aberdeen and any disagreement no matter how trivial, he had to be right. Finally, somebody put one of the tattoos on, washed and rinsed it several times and showed him that it was still there. He knew he was beaten. Then he did something none of us had ever seen before. He apologized to each of us. We looked at each other in stunned silence. Then he went upstairs and never came back to work.

During that same time period Mom's mind was as sharp as a tack but her body was failing her. Negotiating the fifteen stairs to their apartment was becoming more and more difficult and even dangerous as her right knee gave out on more than one occasion.

Dad's solution was to buy her a Stannah chair lift for their 60th anniversary. She loved it. She could sit in the seat, push the button, and ride up or down with ease. She also loved the fact that she could come down to the store and visit us any time she wanted.

Six months later she had the knee replaced. She hated it. Everything healed well and her stubborn Swedishness got her through therapy in record time, but she complained about it constantly.

Her hearing was an issue, too. She complained that she couldn't hear a thing but if I turned the radio in the car to a level that was barely audible to me, she complained that it was too loud. Yet she couldn't hear me when I was looking directly at her and speaking in a drill sergeant's voice.

She had top of the line digital hearing aids but she hated them, too. We all came to dislike them as well. If they weren't placed in her ears correctly they would feed back a high-pitched whistle that had dogs cringing on the next block and us covering our ears. But she couldn't hear it at all.

Dad's driving was getting worse and worse too. Not only had his driving philosophy of letting all the other drivers look out for him caused more than one accident, one of which cost them the front end of their car, he was also forgetting where he was going once he got behind the wheel. Worse, he was forgetting how to get home once he got there. Mom told me how hard she prayed every time they went anywhere, even just to Fairplay, the local grocery store, a block away.

Our solution was to tell him that state law prohibited anyone over ninety from driving. I became their designated driver and spent every Sunday afternoon taking them shopping, out to dinner, or to parties. He still told other drivers to take an alley or go scratch their asses. He would never let the fact that he wasn't driving get in the way of that.

I had a Ford Ranger pickup truck which I would drive to their place. Then I'd take them out in their car, an Oldsmobile Ciera. Dad ended his driving career as an Olds man, just the way he started. In between he'd been a Chevy man, a Plymouth man, and a Chrysler man but his heart was always with Oldsmobile.

This worked out great for a while, but it became more difficult for them to get in and out of their car as the months wore on. We needed something bigger. I sold my Ranger to one of my employees. We sold Dad's Ciera which was eight years old and had only 18,000 miles on it to a friend and bought a 2000 Dodge Caravan. With the sliding side doors and plenty of room between the front and back seats, it was ideal for them. All we needed was a small step stool to help them climb in and out.

Now everything was fine. Mom could use the chair lift to come down to the store to visit her great-granddaughter when Colleen brought her to work. Dad used it, too. He'd come down several times a day, wearing four layers of clothes and a wool cap, complain that it was way too cold in the store, and go right back upstairs. They had a vehicle they could get into and out of easily and plenty of drivers to take them wherever and whenever they wanted to go. Life at Riley's Trick Shop without its founder at the helm settled into a routine.

That changed on Monday, December 3, 2001. Mom came downstairs to visit us and we noticed that her skin was a deep shade of yellow. This must have happened overnight because I didn't notice anything when I took her shopping the day before. Judy took her immediately to Palos Community Hospital where she stayed for a few days for observation and testing.

She had mentioned to her HMO doctor that she'd been having back pains. His response was that she'd never been this age before and she was just experiencing normal aches and pains from aging. He refused to send her for tests. His reason: it would cost him money. We tried to convince her to get away from this quack but she wouldn't listen. Would early testing have helped her? We'll never know for sure. It turned out to pancreatic cancer.

When she went into the hospital the first time, I moved in with Dad to make sure he wouldn't harm himself. It was obvious from the start that was not going to work. Taking care of him and running a business was wearing me out. I needed help. I tried calling an in-home service recommended by a customer but my cell phone kept dropping the call. Someone was looking out for me because the hospital's social worker recommended a company called Polonia, who sent us an angel named Helena.

Helena and her husband Vasily left their children in Ukraine (Yoookrrranyah, as she said it) and came here to find work. A licensed nurse in her native country, Helena could not work as a nurse here because of the language barrier. Her English was much better than my Russian so we had to speak slowly to her and avoid slang or uncommon usage of common words. She and her husband shared an apartment in Chicago but she lived with Mom and Dad during the week and went to see Vasily on Sunday afternoons. She cooked, cleaned and took care of their every need. As I said, she was an angel. Angels don't work for free but I thought eighty bucks a day was a bargain since it allowed me to sleep in my own bed and run my business without having to worry that my parents weren't being properly cared for.

Mom went back into the hospital on December 16 after complaining of intense pain. They told her the cancer was getting worse and there was nothing they could do for her. Dad, Helena, and I came to be regulars at the hospital. Russ, the daytime security guard would always get a wheelchair out for us when I pulled the white Caravan up to the front door. He had it waiting right by Dad's door. It was much too far for him to walk to the cancer ward.

Three days after Mom went back into the hospital we went for our afternoon visit. She wasn't there. Without telling us, she'd decided to fight the cancer and had gone for radiation. It didn't go well and she was never the same. When we saw her again, Helena burst into tears and told me it wasn't good.

Christmas came and went. Mom came home for the last time on December 27. Now she needed round the clock care. I was blessed to have Helena there. When she reluctantly asked for New Year's Eve off to spend with Vasily, I couldn't deny her. Judy stayed with me until midnight and went home. I spent the night with Mom, responding to her requests for morphine and beer. I couldn't deny her, either. It was the first time in years, stretching all the way back to our house on Aberdeen, that I hadn't attended a New

Year's Eve party. I spent the night trying to stay positive by thinking about all those great times, but it couldn't keep out thoughts of what lay ahead. Even though I didn't get much sleep, I spent New Year's Day letting everyone on her massive correspondence list know what was going on.

She died a week later on January 7, 2002.

Mom was not Catholic, but we decided to give her a Catholic funeral anyway. It would be at Dad's church, Our Lady of the Ridge. Their priest was unavailable so they recruited one from another parish. The first thing I told him when he called was that Mom not Catholic. When asked if that would be a problem, he told me his father was a Baptist minister and we'd get along just fine.

The wake was at Blake-Lamb at 112th and Harlem and what a wake it was. Relatives, friends, and former employees showed up from far and wide. Dad didn't have much of a clue of what was going on. Every now and then he'd look at the casket and realize that was "Eleanor up there." One thing he knew for sure was that he was thirsty. When my boys came back from the liquor store with a case or two of MGD, he was very happy. It became a traditional Irish wake and we toasted Mom until the place closed. The funeral director was aghast at all the bottles but we made sure every one was picked up before we left.

The next morning the priest came to say the final prayers at the funeral home. Mom always felt uncomfortable around priests but she would have loved this one. He drove up in a yellow Jeep, wore cowboy boots, black Levis, and a black leather jacket. Standing just a little taller than five feet, he sported long blond hair and a beard to match. He put on one heck of a Mass.

Because of the weather we said our final goodbyes at the chapel at Holy Sepulchre. Three-year-old Courtney asked if that was heaven. When the final prayers were said and the casket taken away, everyone was just milling around but Dad reminded us it was time to go when he his "Let's get the hell out of here" reverberated off the marble walls. When he was finished eating at the funeral luncheon at Garden Chalet on Ridgeland Avenue, he reminded us the same way.

Life goes on and we were back to work the next day. We settled into our new routine of life without Mom. Helena was taking care of Dad. He was oblivious to everything. It seemed to be working well.

Nine days after we buried Mom, I got a call at home from Helena. She was extremely distraught and hard to understand, but I got the idea that she needed help. I was there in minutes. Dad was rolling around the bedroom floor, yelling gibberish. He couldn't walk, either. He calmed somewhat when he realized who I was and we got him back into bed.

Next morning, I was awakened by one of my friends on the Worth Fire Department. Helena had called them when Dad fell after trying to get out of bed again. When I got there, the place was full of firemen fighting to restrain him. He was yelling and unable to walk. I called my friend, Dr. Nick Rizzo, who told me to get him to the hospital as quickly as possible. When Nick asked me who his doctor was, I told him, "You are." I wasn't going to let that HMO doctor kill my father, too.

He must have given everyone a Palos Hospital a hard time because he spent most of the next ten days restrained and sedated. Sometimes he recognized me when I went to see him, other times not. I stopped by every night about supper time and fed him whatever pureed fare the hospital had prepared. He couldn't chew because they had taken away his dental implants. He didn't eat much anyway. Most of the time he appeared to have no clue I was there. He prayed, and called out to Mom and long-dead family and friends.

Over those ten days he was poked, prodded, and tested by doctors, psychologists and psychiatrists. They were stumped. On Friday, February 1, they sent him home. Helena was there to take care of him.

On Sunday morning February 3, 2002, he passed away.

The next morning I was just leaving for the funeral home when a bird flew into the house as I opened the door to the garage. I'm sure Dad had something to do with that. We had never had a bird in the house before. Judy hid in the bathroom and the dog ran outside as I directed our visitor out through the patio door.

The store was open that day. He wouldn't have had it any other way. There were customers but I spent most of the day on the phone with reporters from the Southtown, Chicago Tribune, and the Worth Reporter. Bad news travels fast. When the obituary reporter from the Trib called to ask about

Dad's life, I related some of the stories written here. He told me he rarely gets to laugh in his job and thanked me.

The wake was Tuesday and it was another raucous affair. I've always said a person has had a good life if there was plenty of noise and laughter at his wake. It was obvious Dad had a great life. The place was packed with family and friends, of course, but even more former employees showed up than to Mom's. Even past and present customers came in to offer their condolences and tell stories about the old days on Rhodes, Aberdeen, and Western.

The next morning after everyone else had passed by the casket and the parlor doors were closed, it was just us. I stood there with Judy, our children and their spouses, and our two grandchildren, looking at my Dad lying there with his beloved dollar snatcher, nose blower, snot nose, and a deck of cards. He'd taken them on dozens of trips. We weren't going to allow him to go empty-handed on this one. (I'm certain he'll berate me when we meet again for not selling them instead, but he'd already used the nose blower and snot nose, and the dollar snatcher was one of his worn-out ones.) None of us said a word and no one wanted to be the first to move toward the door. Just as the silence was getting uncomfortable, our grandson, Ethan, unleashed a fart of epic proportions that seemed to reverberate from wall to wall to wall. It was Dad's way of saying, "get the hell out of here and get on with your life."

We burst out of that room laughing so hard our sides ached and tears streamed freely down our faces. The people in the funeral parlor across the hall seemed perplexed but the rest of our family knew. There could be no better final tribute to James Joseph Robert Riley, founder of Riley's Trick Shop, co-founder of Magic Masters of Chicago.

Or maybe there could. A few weeks later there appeared an article in the March edition of the Irish-American Times by Mike Houlihan, writer and performer of the one-man show, "Goin' East on Ashland" and author of "Hooliganism," a collection of his newspaper articles. The following appears there also. Mike summed up in these few words just about everything I wanted to say in this book. When I asked him if I could have the honor of including it, he told me the honor would be his. Thanks, Mike, for the kind words and the nice tribute. Thanks also for helping me fill some more space.

Got a shock one night a few weeks ago when I was perusing the Irish scratch sheet, the obituaries. Jim Riley, owner of Riley's Trick Shop, had finally kicked the bucket at the ripe old age of 93. The Trib ran a photo with the obit and he looked like the same old wisenheimer that used to razz us kids whenever we visited his shop back in the 50s and 60s.

I bought my first fake dog poop at Riley's, as well as the ol' fly in the ice cube, hand buzzers, and several whoopee cushions. We started riding our bikes to Riley's on Saturdays when I was about ten years old. His shop was on 79th Street then and it was a long journey for us kids from 95th Street, but the inventory of corny gadgets kept us rapt for hours afterwards.

On Saturdays the place would be packed with kids cracking up over all the goofy stuff on sale. Riley wouldn't toss you out either. He knew that sooner or later every kid in that store was going to buy something to bring home and embarrass the family. Even if you had a meager allowance you could always afford cigarette "loads." These tiny white slivers of TNT were then inserted into the Lucky Strike of unsuspecting Uncle Charlie. When he lit up his smoke the thing would explode and practically give him a heart attack. Great fun!

As I entered my teens, Riley moved his trick shop to 91st and Western, right next to Jim's Bicycle Shop. I'm sure plenty of kids in my parish said a silent prayer each night thanking Riley for making himself so convenient. You could check out the new bikes at Jim's and then saunter into Riley's for some sure-fire amusement. He had a wall on the left that was covered with rubber masks of every variety, from Khrushchev to the Devil, and plenty of grotesque monsters with eyeballs dangling.

On the right wall up top were the plastic buttocks and boxes and boxes of wacky contraptions, all of them catalogued by Riley. There was something a little bit racy about Riley's, at least to my young eyes. The jokes and tricks were often scatological and that vulgarity just made our gang laugh harder. I once bought a wanted poster and hung it up in my garage until my Dad made me take it down. It offered a $500 reward for some mope who was guilty of "booger picking."

The last time I remember visiting Riley's was right before leaving the old neighborhood for college. I wanted something outrageous to decorate my dorm room and knew exactly where to find it. Riley had a machine that printed fake headlines on a newspaper. It was a very popular gimmick. Riley's wife told me to spell out the headline I wanted on a piece of paper, no more than 28 letters. I wracked my brain for something obscene to print that would greet my new roommate when he walked in the door. Two bucks spent at Riley's could leave an impression that would last a lifetime.

When I handed her the paper, she balked. By today's standards my headline would be every day patter on Leno or Letterman but back in 1967 it seemed crude and tasteless. She called Riley out from the back of the shop and handed him the note with my proposed headline. He looked at it and laughed, and then said, "Print it." He turned to me and squinted through his glasses, "You're a sick kid, ever think about going into the joke business?"

Thirty-five years later I'm in the joke business and Riley is shaking hands with St. Peter. I hope he is using one of his old hand buzzers. God Bless you, Riley.

Mike recently started a radio show on WCEV in Chicago with James "Skinny" Sheahan, the former director of the Mayor's Office of Special Events. It's called "The Skinny and Houli Irish Hour" and airs Saturdays at 3:05 pm at 1450 on the AM dial. The show is pre-recorded, usually at some Irish bar. One week it was at Jack Desmond's in Chicago Ridge, a place my sons and I have frequented on occasion. Since it was so close to our store, Mike asked me to be one of the guests. It went well and I've been back on several occasions. It's always a good time.

A New Beginning

The first weeks and months in the era without Mom and Dad were a blur of going through sixty-five years of accumulated stuff, deciding what to keep and what to do with the rest. Customers and old friends who were just learning the news stopped by to offer their condolences and relate a story or two. At the Magic Masters banquet that year I was presented with an honorary membership to the club. They wanted to keep a Riley on the roster because the name had been associated with the club since its founding in 1944. This non-magician was speechless.

Eventually the apartment was cleaned out. People stopped coming in to the store to offer condolences. Instead they came to see if the place was still open. Rumors had started that it was I who died, Riley's was out of business, and the building had been torn down. I took great joy in dispelling those rumors.

There was no joy in coming in through the back door each morning, though. I missed the sounds of my parents going through their daily activities. I missed stopping up there for a short visit if I had a few minutes. I even missed the feedback of Mom's hearing aids. I actually turned them on a few times just to hear that familiar whistle.

Most of all I missed going up there for supper on nights when I was working late. Judy is an excellent cook who packed me some great meals, but a plate of freshly-cooked food beats anything out of the microwave. Mom claimed to hate cooking but she was really good at it. There was plenty of good conversation, too. I took to sitting alone and reading the Sun-Times or whatever magazine happened to be handy. On top of that, Dad really loved his desserts, or anybody else's if they weren't going to eat them. At many a meal he asked if we could have dessert first. There was always ice cream and cake to follow any meal Mom made.

Many people immerse themselves in their work to take their minds off of the loss of a loved one. I couldn't do that. I was reminded of them every day. There was the deafening silence from their apartment when I came through the back door. Every time I sold an item that Mom had made, I caught a vision of her sitting at her sewing machine or cutting patterns on the dining room table. Dad's horrible spelling was everywhere in signs that he'd made or notes he'd left.

Later that year, our son, Jim, told us his job was going away and asked if he could work for us. We were thrilled. Of course there's always room for another family member in a family business. He could live in the apartment upstairs, too. He was overjoyed with that prospect since he was living in a tiny basement apartment in Lockport. His new digs must have looked like a mansion in comparison. Nothing could bring my parents back but at least there was life again on the second floor.

Blame It On The White Sox

The next few years saw the business settle into a comfortable routine. Halloween business was good, winters were slow, and the rest of the year was steady, if not spectacular. We even managed to get in a few vacations, too.

In 2002, Judy and I went to Canada. There were two reasons for this trip. She'd never seen that part of the world and I wanted to visit my 50th state. Somehow, in all those miles on the road, I'd missed Vermont. It almost didn't happen, though.

As we drove south from Quebec City, we stopped at the US border. It used to be a matter of just telling the border guard you were a U.S. citizen on his way home, and you were on your way. Not so in the post-9/11 world. We showed our passports to the border guard who looked at them and asked why we were driving a car with Connecticut license plates if we live in Illinois. They had a camera that scanned the plates and let him know via a monitor where it thought the plates were from. I assured him they were Illinois plates. He said his monitor said they weren't and refused to physically go look at them. This is what happens when we rely too much on technology. This "are too/are not" exchange went on for what seemed an eternity. Finally, with traffic backed up halfway to the St. Lawrence River, he relented, walked to the front of the car, muttered something, and waved us through.

Another highlight of this trip for me was operating W1AW, the big amateur radio station at the American Radio Relay League headquarters in Newington, Connecticut. To a non-ham this means nothing but, to a ham, it's nothing short of Nirvana. W1AW is the ultimate radio station, with a top-of-the-line transmitter, professional studio microphone, and a humongous beam antenna on a ninety-foot tower. That the transmitter is operated by a two-dollar Radio Shack foot switch doesn't diminish the fact that this is a killer operation.

I'd given some of my ham friends back home a tentative time that I'd be there and what frequency I'd be on. They were waiting. So, it seems, was the rest of the Amateur Radio world. My deal with Judy was that I would operate for one hour. I used every second of that hour and left a lot of disappointed hams without a W1AW contact when I had to sign off.

Two years later we had a family gathering at Disney World. There were three generations of us all together for a week. We hung around the pool, swam in the ocean, and enjoyed each other's company. Our granddaughter, Courtney, celebrated her sixth birthday that week. Through the daughter of a friend, we were able to get her a very small part in one performance of the Lion King show at the Animal Kingdom. No one knows who was more thrilled, us or her.

Between these trips our son, Ed, married Sandi Pisut on a Friday in September of 2004. Ed is a union carpenter. They have three children and live in Lockport, not far from where my mother grew up.

In 2005, Judy and I spent a week at Massanutten in Virginia after touring the battlefields at Gettysburg and Antietam on the way. We spent our time driving through the Blue Ridge Mountains, hiking parts of the Appalachian Trail, and enjoying the Shenandoah Valley.

We expected Halloween that year to be as busy as the ones before. There was no reason not to. As usual, we had attended the Halloween show. As everything came in, we got it displayed in the store and posted on the website. By the middle of October it was obvious this was not going to be a normal Halloween season. The White Sox had had a spectacular regular season and were tearing up the playoffs. No one was out shopping on game nights, especially during the World Series which was the last week in October, normally our busiest week of the year. This Cubs fan was glad to see the Sox take it in four games. Maybe we could salvage something out of our season.

The team had other plans. On Thursday they came home to a heroes' welcome at Midway Airport. That left our store as empty as Wrigley Field in October. Friday was their parade and victory celebration which lasted into the night. With only three days left in October our season was officially a disaster.

We took hope in two things: the Sox might not repeat and we didn't have to order much for the next year because of the abundance of unsold inventory. If we could survive that long, we'd be OK. As any Cubs fan knows, hopes are meant to be dashed. Halloween 2006 was a bigger flop than 2005 but the White Sox weren't in the World Series. What could be keeping everyone away?

We don't get out much in the month of October except to go to work and come home. What we didn't realize that pop-up Halloween shops were everywhere. One Sunday on the way home via Orland Park to get some groceries we noticed at least three of them. Usually they are sponsored by big businesses but sometimes individuals invest some heavy money looking for a quick score in the month of October. The bottom line for us was that we had competition like we never had before.

My apologies go out to the White Sox and their fans. If not for the Cubs, the Sox would be my favorite baseball team. Mullet Night and Elvis Night at US Cellular Field kept us very busy.

Blame It On the TIF

After years of fits and starts, by 2006 the Village of Worth had instituted a TIF district that included our property and most of the commercial property between Ridgeland Avenue and the Tri-State Tollway.

Tax Increment Financing is a method of using future gains in property taxes to finance current improvements which will, hopefully, produce those future gains. Eminent domain is one option a TIF district has. One of the other businessmen in the area told me that we should list the building with a realtor. Setting a price, he said, would protect us against the village if they declared eminent domain.

We had been toying with the idea of selling the building anyway, so, in May of 2007, I called my friend Barry Gaw of Re/Max 10 and put it up for sale. The place had been built specifically with Halloween in mind with more storage space than sales area. What used to be filled with masks, wigs, costumes, decorations, and makeup now sat empty. It was time to downsize. We also thought it would be good to get into an area where there were other retail businesses. Our building sits alone in an area where people don't come to shop unless they're coming specifically to our store. We would worry about where to go when someone bought the building; there are plenty of empty strip malls begging for tenants. Finding a new location wouldn't be a problem.

Selling the building would be. We had plenty of lookers the first year. Most of them didn't realize just how much space five thousand square feet is and walked out saying it was too much building for them. We had a few offers but they were much too low, or so we thought. Had we known about the upcoming recession we'd have accepted them in an instant.

As soon as we put up the For Sale sign, the rumor mill went into high gear again. As with the news of Dad's death they had us going or gone out of business, the building was torn down, there was an empty lot in its place, and I was dead. Once again, I took great joy in proving those rumors false.

Our daughter, Colleen, who follows her grandfather's philosophy of jumping in without testing the water, thought the building would sell right away. She didn't want to be out of a job so she opened her own store. Judy and I tried to explain to her that starting a business in any kind of economy was risky at best. In the current economy it was downright foolish. She'd have none of it. Riley's Trick Shoppe opened at 103 W. Bankview Drive in Frankfort, Illinois in September of 2007. It closed in July of 2010, a victim of the economy and a bigger business wanting her space. She was expecting her third daughter, our ninth grandchild, just before Halloween, too. She worked alone on days when her husband was working his real job. Running a Halloween store by herself with a newborn to take care of was out of the question.

The TIF district had not generated one new building or business within its boundaries.

We thought the tax incentives a TIF offers would be a big help in selling our building but it didn't done much for us or the Village of Worth.

The Evolution of T-shirt Printing: Top of the Food Chain

As December of 2007 approached, the lease on our color copier was coming to an end. Since that was our main way of printing shirts we began to look around at other options. Color copiers are expensive to lease and prone to breakdowns. Despite what the salesmen say, they don't like transfer paper. If it would help them sell a copier, they'd say it would print on sandpaper.

Our inkjet printer was not an option. It did a nice job in a pinch but it was slow and its transfer paper deposited a heavy residue which left a dark shadow on the shirt. That made it stiff and hard to fold. The darker the shirt, the more obvious the residue was.

I looked at desktop laser printers as an alternative because they're cheap enough that we could have two on hand in case one broke down. I thought we could still use laser transfer paper which doesn't leave as much residue as the inkjet paper. Unfortunately, desktop laser printers don't use fuser oil which is a requirement for laser paper. It looked like we'd be getting another color copier with its expensive lease and weekly breakdowns.

Once again, fate intervened. There was a new machine on the market, the GT-541 by Brother. It worked on the same principal as the standard inkjet printers that sit on millions of desktops all over the world but this behemoth weighed in at two hundred pounds and required a special stand to support it. Its ink cartridges were the size of ten standard ones. Instead of using transfer paper, it printed directly on the garment and the print went into the material instead of sitting on top. You couldn't feel it and it would never crack, peel, or fade. There was no area of stiffness or residue like that left by transfer paper. That allowed us to print on darker colors.

We still couldn't print on black, though. The GT-541 had a bigger Brother (pun intended) that did print on black but it cost three times as much and was so big it would require a major retrofit of our building just to get it in the door.

So there you have the evolution of T-shirt printing from hand lettering to one-color printing to full color printing with graphics and photos. We'd come a long way in thirty years.

My Worst Decision Ever

By the spring of 2008 we'd run up a considerable amount of credit card debt trying to keep the business afloat. It was only a matter of time, we thought, before the building would sell, so the plan was to take out a debt-consolidation loan and pay it back with the proceeds once we sold.

So I went to my Friendly Neighborhood Bank (FNB) and had a talk with the loan officer who'd taken care of me since we first started banking there.

For reasons that will become obvious, I will not use the real name of any financial institution or bank associate involved in this story.

Things went well at the start. It was a simple matter to get an appraisal on the building. The paperwork was a relative breeze: fill out a questionnaire and provide a financial statement and two years of tax returns. Despite the recent downturn in our business, the economy was booming and it was only a matter of time before that boom "trickled down" to us, or so we were told. Banks were handing out loans to just about everyone who applied. Our loan officer gave us $50,000 more than we'd requested. The loan would be paid back in three years. No problem, we thought. We'll certainly sell the building in three years. Still, I had to ask.

"If we don't sell the building in that time," I asked the loan officer, "what happens then?"

"We'll renegotiate," he replied with a smile.

I got a bad feeling right then but three years was a long way off. We'd deal with that when the time came.

Adventures In Retail: The Errant Apostrophe

In printing headlines, T-shirts, buttons, and other custom work, I had to deal with a lot of grammatical issues. Sixteen years of Catholic education, especially in the areas of grammar, punctuation, spelling, and usage, drilled into me by some very tough teachers, has turned me into a Grammar Nazi. I can spot an error in those messages that flash at the end of a car commercial. It's a rare day that I don't spot some kind of error in the newspaper. (Disclaimer: as any writer will tell you, the hardest writing to proof is your own. If you, gentle reader, should find any grammatical errors in this text, it's not because I didn't do my very best to make sure everything was perfect. It's because I'm too cheap to send it out to a professional proofreader).

When someone came in with custom printing of any kind, we made them write out what they wanted. We had to deal with some miserable penmanship, some of it worse than mine if that's humanly possible. That usually wasn't a problem unless the customer couldn't read his or her own writing either. Then we just handed it back to them and we worked it out.

The bigger problems were in the area of spelling and punctuation. Misspellings could usually be fixed easily with a look in the dictionary for a word, or the phone book for a name. This was before the internet. Sometimes a phone call would be required but somehow the right spelling could be found in short order.

Punctuation was a different story. There were no easy references. Customers had either forgotten anything they'd learned in grammar school or were never taught in the first place.

The biggest punctuation problem was, and still is, the poor, misunderstood apostrophe. Some people wanted to put one in whenever a word ended in an S. I would explain to them that the apostrophe was used in most cases to show possession or a contraction. Most times they'd see it my way. It must have been my air of academic authority.

There are exceptions to everything, like the man who wanted a headline with the name "Adams" in it. I forget rest of the headline but he wrote the subject of the headline's last name as "Adam's." It was just a name, no possession, no contraction. Besides, possession in this case would put the apostrophe after the S. I explained to him that he didn't need the apostrophe.

"It's the way he writes it," he said.

"You're kidding," I replied.

"Yes he does and that's the way I want it"

"But it's wrong."

Pointing to our sign outside, he said, "Then your sign is wrong."

"No it isn't."

"So why am I wrong?"

"Our name is Riley. Adding the apostrophe and the S shows that the trick shop belongs to us."

Then I opened the dictionary to the list of Presidents and showed him that both John Adams and John Quincy Adams spelled their names without the apostrophe. Knowing that victory was mine, I slammed the book shut and looked up expecting to see defeat in his eyes.

What I saw instead was anger and disgust on a beet-red face with a throbbing vein on its forehead. "I want it the way I wrote it," he snarled through clenched teeth. And that's the way I printed it, knowing that I was right. I just didn't want to be dead right.

Somewhere Brother Collins, my junior year English teacher who used the broken leg of a stool to pound grammar into us, was smiling. It's the only reward I could ever expect. As far as I know there are no medals for defenders of the language.

The "Great" Recession Hits Home

Our store started in The Great Depression. If we survived that, we thought, we could surely survive a recession. We'd done it before. Unfortunately, boom times and trickle-down economics are only a minor help to businesses at the mom and pop level. But when times get bad, all that happens to the boom is that it gets lowered on us and that trickle becomes a torrent, and not in a good way.

Bigger and bigger companies got into the Halloween business and more customers left us to go there and take advantage of their low prices and massive selection. They had huge advertising budgets that we could only dream of. We were like a voice crying in the wilderness so we cut out all advertising and relied on our regular customers to support us.

As Halloweens came and went, our October business got less and less. Our die-hard regular customers told us that we had better prices than the big stores and we really knew the business. The big guys' part-timers didn't know spirit gum from liquid latex. The only result for us was that our Halloween business went down by half every year.

The big bust hurt our Christmas business, too. In the boom years we couldn't give cheap Santa suits away. One time I had set out our top of the line suit, wig and beard set, and all the accessories. The tab came to $750.00. Just as I was about to ring up the customer, another came in the door and said, "That's just what I'm looking for. Set me up." Not a bad half hour's work.

After the bust we couldn't give the good Santa suits away. Our suits came from an American company named Halco out of Pennsylvania. Their suits wear like iron. For the average Santa, twenty years' use isn't out of the question. Only our professional Santas got new suits on a regular basis. People started keeping their suits longer and bought accessories like belts and boot covers as they wore out, instead of replacing the whole set. Those who wanted new suits asked for something cheaper even when we showed them Halco's bottom of the line which included a wig and beard for $85.00. There are cheaper Santa packages out there if you want to wear a flannel or polyester suit with a cheap beard.

It was time to cast a bigger net and start to sell more aggressively on the Internet.

On Road One More Time

Although things had changed a lot, we always tried to make time to get away. It wasn't easy but there are two trips that stand out.

In the fall of 2009 my college roommate, Gary Batchellor, called to invite us to his daughter's wedding. He lives in Batavia, New York, about thirty miles east of Buffalo. Gary's retired so traveling is easy for him, not so much for me. I asked when the wedding was and he told me New Year's Eve.

My response was, "New Year's Eve in Buffalo? Are you nuts?" That was indeed the date. I've known Gary since 1966 so the second question was merely rhetorical. He'd been to all three of my kids' weddings and I owed him, so I said we'd be there, weather permitting. Winter at that end of Lake Erie can be a challenge.

We left on an overcast December 30 and made the trip in the usual nine and a half hours with no problem. Gary put us up for the night and we spent the next day relaxing and talking about our days at St. Joe's. The wedding was beautiful, Gary looked great, Jennifer was radiant, and all the guys in the wedding were in kilts. The food was excellent and they even had pizza delivered at midnight.

We rang in the new year and called Chris and Terri Stella "from the future" because it was 2010 where we were but still 2009 back home. We'd spent New Year's Eve with the Stellas for years and this was our first time not there. We expected to talk to them and the regular gang but everybody was home watching grandchildren. How the times had changed.

The last weather forecast I'd heard before we turned in at 3 a.m. was rain turning to snow later in the day. I got up at 7 and heard they were expecting the snow much sooner. I pulled Judy out of bed, woke Gary up to say good-bye, and we were on the road in half an hour.

They weren't kidding about the snow coming "much sooner." The rain turned to snow as soon as we got past Buffalo and didn't stop until we were west of Toledo.

We made a quick stop at a McDonald's in Erie, Pennsylvania, to grab breakfast. We ate in the car because the snow was coming down at such a rate that we didn't want to lose our ride in a pile of snow in the lot of a sit-down restaurant.

Interstate 90 runs along the southern shore of Lake Erie and the snow was relentless. We found that if we stayed a reasonable distance behind a truck we could keep a steady fifty miles an hour in our Pontiac Vibe. It was still a white-knuckle trip. There was a slight respite from the worst of the weather as the road dipped south to go around Cleveland but the snow came back with a vengeance once we hooked up with I-80.

Somewhere west of Toledo we stopped for gas and I had to scrape an inch of ice from my grill and headlights. We were away from the lake and the sun even came out...for a few minutes. Judy tried to convince herself that the worst was over, but having lived in northwest Indiana for a while, I knew what was waiting for us once we got south of Lake Michigan. As soon as we hit South Bend, it *really* started to snow. Judy wanted to stop but I didn't want to get snowed in for who knew how long.

Obviously, we survived. In spite of everything, we made it home in ten and a half hours.

The next year we decided Christmas was getting out of hand with nine grandchildren. We always have Christmas Eve at our house and the night would find our living room awash in presents. The carpet was later littered with tiny parts of new toys that didn't survive the party and bits of packaging that had eluded the cleaning crew (us). Something had to be done.

We decided that memories are better than stuff so the whole family took a trip together to Orlando. Christmas Eve was still at our house but there were few presents. Each kid got something from Santa and everyone was happy.

The kids left early the following morning and drove through Atlanta's first Christmas Day snow storm in over a hundred years. Judy, her sister, our son Jim, and I flew a day later and got there for Orlando's lowest temperature ever. As the week went on, it got warmer and everybody had a good time.

The kids and their families went to Disney and Universal while the adults sat around the pool and drank margaritas. I spent one day geocaching and we all spent New Year's Eve at the beach.

I never in my life thought I might spend New Year's Eve in the Atlantic Ocean. It was a little chilly, not bad for us but the locals were nowhere to be seen. It was just us Northerners with our pasty white skin. Later the whole family rang in the new year together.

In subsequent years we all went to Great Wolf Lodge and The Wilderness in Wisconsin Dells. One year we rented a house in Galena and went tobog-ganing. Aunt Sandi landed awkwardly on her saucer sled and injured her ankle. Aunt Kristen saw her son, Jake, lose his boot on the way down the hill. She took off on a plastic sled and went airborne over a mogul, but still grabbed the boot and handed it to Jake when she reached the bottom of the hill. You can't put colored paper and a shiny bow on stuff like that. We'll continue these trips as long as we can. Gifts are nice but memories last a lifetime.

Leave Me A Loan

By the winter of 2011 it was obvious we'd be unable to pay back the loan on the building. I called my loan officer and we got the negotiations rolling.

During the term of the loan, the Friendly Neighborhood Bank was taken over by some large East Coast institution called the POS Bank. Obviously, that's not the name but it's a good description. The staff at the FNB remained the same and not much had changed other than the name, but things were different beneath the surface. Once I got the paperwork for the new loan I found out just how different. Not only did I have to get an appraisal and supply the standard two years of tax returns, I had to fill out their balance sheet. They couldn't accept the one I'd supplied previously from Quick Books. It had to be done on their form.

Column One required me to supply a balance sheet for the previous year. No problem. Column Two required one for the entire current calendar year, not easy because it was only February. Column Three wanted me to peer into the future and come up one for the following year. The crystal ball was broken but I did the best I could. Six weeks later I turned in a giant sheaf of paperwork and waited.

As the time was drawing short, my loan officer stopped by on a Monday to say that everything was going well and we should be signing the renewal shortly. That Friday I called him with a question and got his voice mail. I called again the following Monday and was told that he was no longer an employee of the mighty POS bank. When I asked who was in charge of my loan now, I was told they had no record of a loan.

Fortunately, I'm a believer in CYA and had made copies of everything. I turned them in and thus began a lesson in dealing with the new world of post-recession banking.

At first they were reluctant to even look at the paperwork, let alone give us a loan. I never did figure out why. For the previous thirty-six months we'd made every payment. Maybe some were a little late during the winter when business was slow, but we always made them up. Finally, they gave us a six-month extension while they figured out their next move.

Around Town

Dealing with the POS bank made for a miserable 2011. One phone call changed things for the better, at least for a couple of days.

I got that call On October 5 from a producer at Channel 9, WGN here in Chicago, asking if we'd like to be on their Around Town segment the following Tuesday. Every morning they sent a crew to a remote location and broadcast live from there in the seven and eight o'clock hours. I agreed before they finished asking.

This was our third attempt with WGN. The first was April Fool's Day 1997 when I was already booked with Fox Thing In The Morning. The next time was in March of 2003 but we got preempted by the invasion of Iraq. We hoped nothing would keep the third time from being the charm.

On Sunday, Judy and I went in to straighten everything and make it look like we had a lot of stock. We did have a lot of stock but it needed to be better organized. I cleaned the T-shirt printing area like it was brand new. Judy filled the holes in the costume area and filled or faced every spot on the shelves. The place looked great when we left. We hoped Monday's customers wouldn't mess it up too much.

Monday was Columbus Day, the unofficial kickoff to the Halloween season when we started staying open until 8 p.m. every weekday. It was busy but the place still looked good by closing time so we headed home to hit the rack early.

The alarm went off Tuesday at 5 a.m. and I was on the road by 5:40 after a bite of breakfast and doing the best I could to look good for the camera. On the way I passed an open field where the setting moon cast an unearthly glow to the miasma hugging the ground. That alone was worth getting up for. I pulled into the parking lot at 5:58 and the WGN truck followed one minute behind me. The camera operator showed up twenty minutes later, and Ana Belaval herself fifteen minutes after that.

WGN's Ana Belaval, Jim Riley, and granddaughter Courtney Jage

Anyone who's seen Ana on the air knows she's a real high-energy ball of fire. She doesn't stop while the camera's off either. We had four segments each hour consisting of long and short teases and a three-minute interview. Between each segment she was looking for things to show the viewers, asking questions, and giving directions to all involved. She didn't stop for the entire two hours. She really enjoyed my children and grandchildren who were there to model costumes, since Halloween was the main focus of the day.

She had a ball going through all the drawers looking for gimmicks. She liked the electronic fart machine but really loved the butt shorts, a pair of boxer shorts with a fake rubber butt on the back. She put them on and loved shaking that thing for the camera. We loved watching her do it. They really liked it back at the studio, too.

All too soon it was over. The crew went on to their next assignment and Ana headed back to the station to prepare for the next day's Around Town.

After everyone left, Judy, Jim, and I had an hour until it was time to open for business and we wanted to head out for a well-deserved breakfast. One mope had followed the TV wire through the open front door and wouldn't leave. He didn't by anything either. He just wanted to stand around. We were famished but tried to be subtle. Subtlety didn't work so we explained the situation but he was still unmoved. Finally, the tried and true "get the hell out of here" worked like a charm. The waitress in the Worth Diner down the street recognized us and said we looked good on TV. We'd made the big time.

When we got back to the store we noticed that Ana had left her jacket. I sent it back to her at the station with the note: "Ana, Tuesday was a lot of fun, but you have to stop leaving your stuff at my place." I hope that didn't get her in trouble.

Did it help us? It's hard to tell. In the short term, several people came in to let us know that they were in the store because they'd never heard of us until they saw us on Channel 9. One lady drove all the way from Niles because she saw a T-shirt design she liked on the wall behind me. I hoped they would turn into repeat customers and tell their friends.

The Axe Man Cometh

On a snowy January 20, 2012, we decided to open just in case some intrepid customer needed a last-minute whoopee cushion. The snow was coming down so hard that our plow guy didn't even come to do the lot.

Jim said he'd take care of the store since he didn't have to travel, but I had nothing to do and came in anyway. We spent the day talking about his upcoming wedding. My son, who we never thought would get married, was finally tying the knot. He had reconnected with Bridget Plumlee, who was in his class at Lockport High School. She and her two kids, Tyler and Samantha, had moved in with him upstairs. It sure was nice to hear all that activity up there again.

We were just about ready to call it a day when a car pulled into the lot. At last we would hear the register ring.

It wasn't to be. The "customer" turned out to be a representative from the POS Bank. We'll just call him… On second thought, you don't want to know what I'd like to call him. Let's refer to him as The Axe Man. He came to tell me that POS Bank was not going to renew our loan. At least he had the decency to tell me to my face instead of doing it via phone or email. Of course, I tried to get him to reconsider but he was unmoved.

The Axe Man left and I went home in the snow to deliver to bad news to Judy.

Over the next few months I tried to get a loan from other banks but once one bank turns you down, they all do. Thus began a series of stalling tactics, anything to keep us going until we could find a buyer for the building or some other way to stay in business.

God Bless the Broken Road

No one in our family ever thought he would marry, but the big day came for our son Jim in March of 2012.

The big day was also the Saturday before the South Side Irish parade on Western Avenue in Beverly. That was one of our biggest T-shirt printing days as everyone proclaimed to the world on their backs and chests what drinking team they were on and how drunk they were going to be. Due to the rowdiness of previous years, the parade was suspended for three years. Now that they had brought it back and all the T-shirt business with it, I wasn't thrilled about losing half a day's business, but my son was getting married. Family trumps business any day. We made it known that we would be closing early and hoped for the best.

It was a very good day and customers seemed to have gotten the message. My daughter Colleen had come in to help. She worked the counter and I spent four hours straight at the T-shirt machine. By two o'clock things had died down and it was time to head off to the church.

The wedding was scheduled for four o'clock in the small sanctuary of LaGrange Christian Assembly in, you guessed it, LaGrange. The hour before was a flurry of activity with greeting guests and lots of photographs. Our friend, Don Pointer, a great wedding photographer, and his wife Nora presented us with their services as a wedding gift to Jim and Bridget. As the time for the ceremony was drawing near, Don realized that he didn't have a picture of the whole family. With ten minutes left and the pastor breathing down his neck, he frantically started getting the entire family together for a group shot. In three minutes he had all twenty-one of us posed and photographed.

The entire Riley clan, in no particular family
grouping, at Jim and Bridget's wedding
(Photo by Donald W. Pointer)

We scrambled to our seats and the ceremony began precisely at 4, right on time. Pastor Hal Kooistra conducted a beautiful ceremony based on talks with Jim and Bridget. It was a perfect balance of humor, seriousness, and readings from scripture. Jim's brother Ed sang "The Broken Road" by Rascal Flatts. And all our children were finally married.

We moved to the all-purpose room which is normally set up for Sunday services by that time on Saturday. That afternoon it was full of round tables with seating for eight, with white table cloths and floral centerpieces.

Jim is an avid Bulls fan and he wanted the bridal party to be introduced the same as the team is at the Madhouse on Madison. Tommy Edwards couldn't make it so the job fell to me. Everyone was seated, the lights dimmed, and the familiar twanging guitar of ELO filled the hall. The church has a killer sound system so even I sounded great as I brought in the bridal party with, "Aaaaaaaaaand now...the starting lineup for your Team Riley." Bridget's

Dad, Don Plumlee, read the invocation, her daughter Sam read a poem, and it was time to feast.

As emcee I explained how dinner was going to work. "What we have for you is a sit-down dinner: you go down both sides of the long table to my left, get your food, go back to your table, and sit down." That long table was loaded with just about anything you could want, most of it provided by Judy and her sisters. It was wonderful as usual. Guests went back multiple times and there was nothing left.

There was no booze, no DJ, and we had to clear out by 8 o'clock so the church crew could clean up and prepare the room for Sunday services. Still, people told us for months after that this was the best wedding they'd been to in a long time. The whole thing, including tuxes, cost less than and thousand dollars.

The Final Battle, Part One

The rest of 2012 was the usual blur of birthday parties, work, and all the other activities that go with having a large family. There were two highlights. Our grand-daughter Courtney became the first of the new generation to graduate grade school. Of course, that was the cause of much celebration.

Fifty years prior to Courtney's graduation from Manhattan Junior High I graduated from St. Sabina's and the class of 1962 was having a reunion. The committee had formed in July of the previous year and I was part of it from the beginning. It was great getting together with some people I hadn't seen since graduation day. We planned and discussed but mostly we laughed. It was like no time had passed.

The reunion at Gaelic Park was in November and was well-attended. There was a great dinner; some nice video; a remembrance of classmates who had passed; plenty of hugs, kisses, and handshaking; and laughter, lots of laughter.

Those were some great times but the looming loss of our building in Worth cast a pall over the entire year. What were we going to do about the POS Bank and their legion of doom? If we couldn't sell the building there would be no chance of repaying the loan. After the financial disaster of 2008 and its repercussions, the only way a bank was lending money was to those who could prove they didn't need the loan in the first place.

After forty years the building was showing its age and would need a lot of work. The few people who had come to look at it either didn't realize how big five thousand square feet really is or they knew how much work it would be to repair and retrofit to their purposes. Others who seemed interested backed out because they couldn't scrape enough together for the down payment or get a loan.

One very interested party wanted us to "hold paper" on the building. That means we would be the bank and he would make mortgage payments to us after we moved our business out and his moved in. This sounds great in theory. If his business folded, however, we'd be stuck with an unsellable building and on the hook for the property taxes with no way to generate any income to pay them. Over the next thirty years, or whatever term the loan turned to be, we'd have to worry about every month's payment. We'd have that hanging over our heads until we were in our nineties. We were desperate but not that desperate.

I'd spoken to lawyers and financial counselors but there appeared to be nothing we could do. "You're screwed," was their usual response. We were able to protect our home and other assets. I moved our money out of the POS Bank before they froze our accounts. Beyond that, we really were screwed. Everything we'd worked for our entire lives was about to go away. There would be no chance of retirement.

I had stalled the bank as long as possible by asking again and again for a little more time to sell the building. We haggled over short-term loans but they always fell through. The bank didn't want another unsellable property on their books and they let us draw things out as long as possible, hoping as we did, that someone would buy the building and resolve the issue. As 2012 became 2013 our backs were against the wall. The POS bankers were leaning on us and there was nothing to do but let them foreclose.

Why Own When You Can Rent?

When we finally realized we weren't going to get anything near what we were asking for the building, we looked at the possibility of moving to a smaller space. It was becoming painfully obvious that even if we were able to sell, we'd never have enough to retire from the sale of the building alone. The thinking was that if we moved to a strip mall we would be near other businesses and maybe we could get some new customers that way. With foreclosure looming, that plan moved directly to the front burner.

Over the winter of 2013 I got a real schooling in renting business property. Most places list their rent on an annual basis. The average guy like me considers rent to be a monthly expense so a place showing a rent of $36,000 seems insane until you break it down to the monthly cost of $3,000. That's just the rent. Then it gets even crazier. They add on property tax, insurance, and CAM (Common Area Maintenance). The common area is any part of the property not inside the renter's unit. Now the monthly rent bill goes from $3,000 to $4,500 or more. And any work they do on the property that costs them over and above your CAM input is dumped on you at the end of the year. If they decide to repave the parking lot, the renter is on the hook for a share based on the square footage he's renting. Some places I looked at triple their rent for October, November, and December.

In spite of all those obstacles it was time to start looking again. Instead of driving around, blocking traffic, and telling other drivers to "go scratch yer ass," I took the 21st century approach and used the internet. Let me tell you, rent is expensive. It doesn't matter where. Orland Park, Tinley Park, Palos Heights, nothing is what I would consider affordable. Sure, we could lower the cost by renting something small but then we'd have to cut our product line.

I set up some standard storefront sizes on the computer; drew in our show cases, display racks, and a stockroom; and designed a new printing area that gave us plenty of T-shirt storage, room to move without running into each other, and space to grow. I set up different configurations and came up with a minimum of 1,500 square feet. That would be tight. Closer to 1,800 would be ideal. If we need extra short-term storage, there was room in our basement.

Then the search began in earnest. Most places were in the 1,700 square foot range. If they weren't prohibitively expensive, there were other reasons to look elsewhere: there was no parking, visibility was bad, or the place was a dump.

One night my son Jim called and told me he'd found a place. As soon as he gave me the address I knew exactly where. My daily commute took me right past it morning and night but I'd never given it a thought. I knew it was there but never even had an occasion to pull into the parking lot. A closer inspection showed that there were three businesses to the east, and one to the west. Even though the place we were looking at was at the back of a huge parking lot, there were two active businesses and a sign near the street. As an added bonus, it was right across from a high school. It just might work.

The first time we went inside, it wasn't pretty. There were ceiling tiles missing and the ones that were still in place had water stains. The previous tenant had left holes in the wall. The floor was bare cement. This was in February. With no gas or electric service, it was cold, damp, dark, and uninviting even though the low winter sun pounded through the front windows. I didn't know how it was going to work at any price.

Oh yeah, price. Just what was this going to cost us? The only way to find out was to submit a letter of intent along with the required financials, and wait. After some negotiating, we agreed to a five-year lease at just over a dollar a square foot on about 2,500 square feet of space, including taxes, insurance, and CAM. After all my research, a buck a square foot for rent was an offer no one could refuse. Throw in the extras and it was a no-brainer. Riley's Trick Shop's fifth location would be 8086 W. 111th Street in Palos Hills.

At the end of the five years, Judy and I would be close to maxing out our Social Security. There's no big, fat pension waiting when you walk away from a mom and pop business. We would call it a career and Jim could take over. That was the plan. I should have called to mind those words of Robert Burns about the best laid plans.

The Beginning of the End

We had been planning for the move as soon as we'd put the building up for sale, but the attempts to throw out, recycle, or sell anything we couldn't bring with us were half-hearted at best. Now we had a lease on a new location that started on the first of May and it was already March.

Anyone can tell you that after staying in one place for a long time, you accumulate a lot of stuff. We'd been in Worth for almost forty years. We had tons of stuff, five thousand square feet of it, to be exact, and it had to fit into half that area. We needed to downsize—quickly.

Jim had inherited a Ford F-150 pickup truck from Bridget's step-father. It proved invaluable as he loaded it with all kinds of things headed for the boneyard. Even though he sometimes made two trips a day with its eight-foot bed loaded side to side and front to back all the way to the cap, it seemed to hardly make a dent.

While he was doing that, I began taking down the hundred feet of angle-iron shelving that ran down the west side of the store. Before I could even start, everything had to be moved off the top shelves and the drawers on the bottom had to be moved out. Then a tough job got tougher because there were three levels of plywood shelves that had to be taken off even before I began working on the metal supports. Every nut and bolt was assembled my Jim Wallace, my Dad, and me. They were tightened to last a long time. I'm sure those two were laughing and pointing at me as I fought to take the whole thing apart by myself. It became an almost round the clock operation.

We were still open for business and Judy took care of the counter. Jim and I had to stop what we were doing and help if she got busy or if there were T-shirt and headline customers. We had to apologize for the way we looked but the job had to be done and we still needed to make a buck while doing it. Fortunately, nobody seemed to mind.

Only the POS Bank minded. The original axe man was a mere lackey of the bank. We had been kicked up the chain to our new tormentor, one of their minions. He told me the bank was going to save us the hassle of foreclosure and instead would accept what sounded to me like a "DeeDinLoo" from us. I called Barry Gaw, my realtor, and he told me the banker was talking about a Deed in Lieu of Foreclosure or a Deed in Lieu for short. Yes, this would save us from a long, drawn-out foreclosure but, once we turned the deed over, we'd have to pay rent to the bank. The thought of paying even one more dime to the POS Bank was revolting, but the Deed in Lieu was the only option.

For the next month all I did was take down shelving, move drawers, take care of customers, and deal with the minion on the phone. I never met him in person which explains why I'm not writing this from prison. We haggled over when we'd transfer the deed, how much rent we would grudgingly fork over, and when it would begin. The discussions got more and more intense but I had lost the will to fight and acceded to his demand that we would begin paying rent on the first of May. May Day, indeed.

As April turned to May, the tear-down continued. Beaten down in body and mind, I prayed for a well-placed tornado to sweep it all away some time while the building was empty…unless the minion from the bank was there alone.

Time To Move On, One Last Time

On the first of May I got the keys to the new location. They had done a nice job of fixing it up. The gaps in the ceiling tiles had been filled, the water-stained tiles replaced, and the floor had brand-new carpeting. It wasn't the greatest but we'd never had carpeting before. The original store had a wood floor and the other stores had tile over cement. Walking on something soft had a certain allure to it.

The two units we'd rented totaled just over 2,500 square feet, two thousand of which made up the sales area. Some customers thought it was bigger, others thought it was smaller than the sales area in Worth. It actually was bigger by about three hundred square feet but the customer is always right. I didn't argue with any of them.

In this vast area of empty space was a lonely chair that the previous tenants had left. It was nothing fancy, just a gray, padded, armless, stackable chair with a bent leg. I straightened the leg and sat down to survey the future home of Riley's Trick Shop in an attempt to figure out how we were going to fill all this empty space. I had been simulating layouts in the computer but there's nothing like looking at the real thing. This was going to be a huge job.

Back in Worth, the tear-down continued. I was still working on the shelving but now I had a place to bring some of the drawers. That afternoon the move began and continued until June 20th.

Hardly a day went by without one or more of us filling a vehicle and moving something or other.

During all this, Jim and Bridget were buying a house and their move coincided with the store's. He was working twice as hard between moving recyclable items from the store to Metro Recycling in Blue Island by day and furniture and personal items to his new digs in Midlothian by night.

The store's real move began on Sunday May 19. Jim and I, along with my sons-in-law, Roger Jage and Al Gioia, rented a truck and moved the glass show cases, lots of the drawers from the stockroom, almost all of the dismantled angle iron shelving, and the button machine to the new place. That took two trips and most of the afternoon. We made all our business transactions on folding tables over the next week.

On the following Saturday, May 25th, the building in Worth began to die. That was when we took down the "nonsense" plaque that had been there for the last forty years. It didn't go without a fight. The bolts were so rusted and worn that neither a wrench nor a screwdriver would work. We were able to pry two of them out and one broke but the last one had to be cut with a hacksaw blade shoved behind the plaque. Half an hour and several scraped knuckles later, the building in Worth was just that, a building. It was no longer Riley's Trick Shop. We closed for business for the last time at three that afternoon.

After a much-needed Memorial Day holiday we got serious about moving. Jim and Bridget were at the Worth store at six Tuesday morning and had most of the metal shelving behind the counters down by the time I got there. For the next three weeks all we did was disassemble, pack, move, and reassemble. For the rest of the big items, I rented another truck on Sunday, June 9, and my son Ed came to help.

We made our first sale at the new store the Wednesday after Memorial Day. No one remembers what it was or who bought it. What surprised us most was that we had what the customer wanted and could actually find it.

The old store was becoming an empty shell and the new one was taking shape. I was building new counters out of the old angle iron. That would form our newer and bigger T-shirt department. I was assembling our new gridwall rack displays. Originally, I wanted ten of them but cooler heads prevailed and we wound up with eight. It took a whole hour to put one these things together. It was a major workout but all that empty space was filling in.

The Final Battle, Conclusion

I had agreed with the POS Bank to pay rent beginning May first on the building in Worth and they leaned hard on me because I wasn't forthcoming with the money. A new wrinkle had developed, one that might keep the cash in our hands. The bank didn't see it that way and the pressure was mounting. The minion was calling multiple times a day. He never let me speak and, if I tried to get a word in edgewise, he'd interrupt before I could get a complete sentence out.

I'd had a stent installed two years before to alleviate a blockage in a cardiac artery. As a cardiac patient I told him he was just aggravating my condition and to never call me again. We would do everything via email. It still pissed me off when I saw his name multiple times in my inbox but at least I could write what I wanted to without being interrupted.

The new wrinkle was Barry Gaw's bringing a prospective buyer—a last-minute savior. Most people Barry had brought were the kind who would gape, ask a few questions, pace off a couple of areas, or even talk about how they would utilize a certain space. This man was different. He seemed truly interested and eventually made an offer. Instead of turning the building over to the bank, we thought we just might avoid foreclosure and actually walk away with some seed money for the new store.

Two words: yeah, right. He had taken samples of the floor tile and the roofing for testing. On June third he called Barry to tell him what we already knew—both tested positive for asbestos.

According to the Riley Theory of The Way Things Ought to Be, asbestos flooring wouldn't be a big deal. Asbestos is not a health issue unless it's broken down into microscopic fibers that can be breathed deep into the lungs and accumulate over many years. We had walked on that tile and worked under that roof for almost forty years. I had spent three days laying that tile, handling it with my bare hands. Not one of us has any of the diseases associated with asbestos.

In my perfect world the tile could be sealed and a new floor put over it. The roof could be left alone. Unfortunately, our building wasn't in a perfect world. It was in Cook County and the asbestos situation would have to be remediated. That meant it would have to be removed under hazmat conditions and completely replaced.

We thought for sure that the buyer would back out. He didn't, but remediation destroyed any chance of our walking away with any kind of compensation for the building.

During one of my daily email chats with the POS Bank, the minion made the comment that the bank was going to take a $30,000 hit on this deal. A hit that size for the POS Bank is like a mosquito bite on an elephant's ass. For us it meant a whole lot more and I told him so in words better left drifting somewhere in cyberspace.

Despite his threats and demands for the rental payments for May and June, we never did pay the POS Bank a cent. I considered that a moral victory but he bank got in one parting shot at the closing on June 20th. The sales agreement laid out where the buyer's money would go. One line listed the bank's piece of the action. Another showed how much Barry would get and another showed what they were paying a lawyer they had hired for us. As a final thumbing of their nose at me, one line read: **THE SELLER GETS NOTHING.**

Through all this the buyers were stand-up people. They never complained about all the stuff we left and even said they'd call us if they found anything they deemed important. They did and held it for us until we could come and get it. When they replaced the sign outside, they saved our **RILEY'S TRICK SHOP** panels for us. One we put up in the Palos Hills store until we closed. It's now in Jim's garage. The other panel is in the back yard of Dirk Spence, also known as Mr. D of Mr. D's Magic and Illusion Show.

Our former building is the new home of Suburban Truck Parts. They did a lot of work on the old building and it looks great. May they enjoy many happy and successful years there.

My Turn

The closing date of June 20th was looming large like the grille of a speeding semi in our rearview mirror. It was obvious that we'd never have the building cleared out in time. After Jim and Bridget moved everything of theirs to their new house, we realized just how much there was of my parents' things left. Apparently we hadn't cleaned out the upstairs as well as we thought after they died. Add that to what was downstairs in the store and we had a monumental task before us.

We tried selling some things on Craig's List and had a little luck, but it made neither a dent in our pile of stuff nor a bulge in our wallets. We fared little better trying to give stuff away.

What bothered me most was that we couldn't give away my mother's electronic organ. It was her pride and joy. We got a few calls but nobody was interested after learning how heavy it was and that it would have to be brought down fifteen steps. I hope the new owners found a use for it.

Under the shelving and drawers in the stockroom there was an archeologist's delight. Forty years of things had fallen behind the drawers. There were all kinds of old signs and price stickers, items we hadn't carried in years, remnants of dry-rotted balloons, and countless papers with notes and lists. Some of the writing was as clear as the day it was written. When I recognized whose hand it was, a face came to mind and with it a memory of happier times.

Everywhere those shelves had been there was dust so thick it could be picked up at one end and a pile several feet long would follow. It had lain undisturbed for decades. As I sucked that mass in to my shop vac, I realized that I was vacuuming up bits of myself, my wife and kids, my parents, our employees, and the thousands of customers who had supported us over the years. I thought of them all as the vacuum droned on.

My daughter Kristen had taken her grandmother's vanity that Dad had found in the alley back on Rhodes Ave. It's been restored to its original glory. Colleen took her grandma's shadow box and a couple of pieces of antique furniture for restoration.

The rest was up to me and it was decision time. As the days drew short we started earlier in the morning and worked later in the evening but there just wasn't enough time to get it all. We had to prioritize. Some things that had been part of my entire life had to be left behind.

The closing was set for two p.m. so there was time that morning for a couple more trips. It was Jim, Colleen, and me for the very last one. His truck was full, Colleen's van was full, and my car was so full I couldn't see out the back window. I had to hold stuff out of the way just to use the gearshift.

As morning was rolled toward afternoon, we went back inside to take another look for anything we couldn't leave, any sliver of some treasured item we could squeeze in somewhere. We soon realized we'd done all we could and it was time to go. As the last echo of our voices bounced off the empty walls, my son and daughter stopped and stared at me. That last time we'd moved, Colleen was three and Jim hadn't been thought about yet, but they knew the tradition.

"Aren't you gonna say it?" they asked.

"What?" I replied. "Oh, yeah. Let's get the hell out of here."

111th Street in Palos Hills

Another New Beginning

Once the moving was done, we spent the final week of June 2013 putting the finishing touches on the new store. It became official when we mounted the "nonsense" plaque. Due to the lack of space and the fact that we didn't own this building, we couldn't mount it on the wall outside. It was inside, away from the weather, but still greeting customers as it had on Western Ave. and in Worth. Riley's Tricks and Gifts was officially in its new home.

That's right. We changed our name to show that we were also providing gifts in addition to tricks. Most of our custom-printed T-shirts, mouse pads, and coffee mugs were purchased as gifts. We had an extensive selection of over the hill gifts. We were also a full-service advertising specialty supplier and the bulk of those items were printed as giveaways. We were definitely a trick *and* gift shop. It was Jim's idea that we change the name to reflect that. It never caught on with customers and even he reverted to calling it Riley's Trick Shop.

We had expected to take a hit the first couple of months we were in Palos Hills. You don't just pull up stakes after four decades in one spot and not cause "a great disturbance in The Force" as one customer put it. A lot of people called in a state of panic. "Where are you?" or "Did you move?" was the first thing we heard after answering the phone. Our phone number hadn't changed and our website and Facebook pages were still active, but with the new information. We weren't difficult to find…unless you tried Google maps. They had us in Sacred Heart Church's parking lot across the street. We advertised extensively, too.

One man who apparently didn't have a cell phone and had never heard of the internet came storming in the door one morning yelling, "I can't believe you moved and didn't say anything. I've been driving around for hours."

Damn! I knew there was someone I forgot to tell.

"Well, you've found us," I said, "Now what can I do for you?"

As if he hadn't heard me he yelled, "You gotta put up some kinda sign at your place in Worth."

"It's not our building anymore," I said with a little more edge in my voice.

"Still, you gotta put up a sign over there."

I tried to explain that I couldn't put up a sign on a building that I didn't own but he kept insisting that I had to. This give and take went on for a few more rounds before the other customers got upset and told him to shut up. For all his anger about our not being at the old place, he never did buy anything. But he did leave us with one parting shot, "You gotta put up a sign over there."

One customer beat me to it and told him to get the hell out of there.

The good folks at Suburban Truck Parts were very helpful with wayward Riley's customers and gave them all the information they needed to find us. They just had to go inside and ask. This man obviously did not.

One of my friends walked in the front door at the old place and, not noticing the new sign or the completely different layout inside, stepped up to the counter and asked for me. Old habits die hard.

It wasn't long after this that a man came in, looked around for a few minutes and said, "I wish you a lot of luck. This mall seems to be the place where businesses go to die." The Prophet of Doom had spoken.

Even though the first two months were very good, things slowed down in August. "It'll get better once school starts," we said, nodding toward Stagg High School, right across the street. When school was back in session and nothing happened we said, "It'll pick up once we have our grand opening."

Our grand opening was Saturday October 5, 2013, a cloudy, humid day with an afternoon storm. We had advertised heavily and spent weeks stocking and making the place look especially nice. That morning we hung a big **GRAND OPENING** sign across our front window and moved a couple of the gridwall racks outside (they were on wheels) to show our wares to passersby. People started showing up as soon as we opened and kept coming all day. Unfortunately, the bulk of them were family and friends. We provided snacks and drinks but our grandchildren made short work of them.

Maybe the Prophet of Doom was right. Our grand opening wasn't so grand after all.

Hunka Hunka Burning Jimmy

Even an appearance by the legendary Jimmy Elvis himself couldn't save our grand opening. Once we settled in Palos Hills we were just a few blocks away from his home and became one of the stops on his daily rounds. We used to see him in Worth if he could bum a lift from his sister or a friend, or ride his bike when the weather was nice. It seemed that every time we saw him he had a new bike. When asked what happened to the old bike and he'd come back with the same answer: "I took it back to Walmart's." I wrote about characters in an earlier chapter, but Jimmy Elvis is the character of characters.

For anyone in the Palos and Worth areas no explanation of Jimmy Elvis is necessary. For those who have not had the pleasure of meeting him or seeing him "perform", no explanation will do. I'll give it a try anyway. The short story is that Jimmy was taken in by a loving family despite his many challenges. They nurtured him the best they could. Eventually he went to work for the Post Office, retired, and is living on a federal government pension.

Jimmy's claim to fame is that he thinks he's an Elvis impersonator. There is at least one other Jimmy Elvis out there but ours has developed a singular style that makes him stand out from the crowd. He is THE Jimmy Elvis. What he lacks in singing talent and the ability to remember lyrics, he more than makes up in enthusiasm as he dons his Elvis jumpsuit, cape, and wig and sings karaoke with the innocence and unaffected zeal of a child. He has more than one CD in circulation, he's been on the Mancow radio show in Chicago, and he's been written up in a multi-page spread in the Southtown Star. He truly is the real deal.

Except for Elvis night at Sox Park, Jimmy was our biggest Elvis para- phernalia customer. He had us make countless T-shirts with photos of him in his costumes or proclaiming himself to be the "Number One King, Legend, Superstar" or the "New King of 'Rocking' Roll." There is no way to know how many Elvis wigs, capes, scarves, crowns, or jumpsuits he bought from us over the years.

On one visit he wanted a new Elvis jumpsuit but all we had was a medium. That's two sizes too small for him. He held it up and insisted it would fit. Over the years we'd found that there was no arguing with him so I told him to take it into the bathroom and give it a shot. I thought he'd realize it was never going to fit and just give up. Not Jimmy. Not only did he get it on but he proudly came out to show us. It's a good thing it was just my son and me in the store as Jimmy strutted out in that white jump suit. It was stretched to the brink of transparency and we saw things we will never be able to unsee. We had let him try it on because it was unsellable due to some missing some parts. Jimmy obviously wasn't missing any parts so we told him he could have it for nothing if he'd just go back and change—quickly.

Sometimes characters can get on your nerves like Crazy Jim back in Worth who claimed to be the late Robert F. Kennedy or others who claimed to be followed by aliens or government spies.

Then there are those who are upset by some little thing and are more than willing to give an earful to anyone within shouting distance. After the law was passed that banned car dealers from being open on Sunday, one customer ranted about how inconvenient that was for him, like he buys a car every Sunday. In our later years we had to listen to the Obama haters and how the President was personally responsible for everything that was wrong in their lives.

Jimmy Elvis wasn't like that. He would just go on and on about how he was the new king of "rocking" roll, how he wasn't the king, how he wanted to be king, or how he didn't want to be king. It got old after a while. Other times he'd burst into an Elvis performance that made adults laugh and children cringe. It was at those times that we'd tell him, nicely, that it was time to go.

Then he'd shuffle in off in his slow but steady gait and let us know he'd be back the next day with a hearty, "See ya tamarrh!"

Well, there is no more "tamarrh", at least not for us. Jimmy Elvis could be annoying at times and could stomp on anyone's last nerve but he had a good heard and never meant any harm. He's probably still shuffling his rounds on 111th. I wonder if he misses us. God Bless Jimmy Elvis.

The Best-Laid Plans

The plan when we moved to Palos Hills was for the three of us, Judy, Jim, and me, to go on unemployment until the store generated enough business for us to start paying ourselves again. After the first two months, it appeared we could start doing that by the end of the year. Then things started to taper off. Halloween was only half what it was in Worth and Christmas wasn't much better. We had to try something else.

Our internet business had been slumping, too, so I thought we could start selling on Amazon. Maybe casting a wider net would help generate more income. To get an idea of what we were going up against, I started nosing around Amazon.com looking for other businesses that were selling the same products we did. That's when I found out why our internet business had taken a dive. Those businesses were selling exactly the same things we did, but for less than they cost us. They offered free shipping, too. How could they do that? We bought direct from the importer or the manufacturer. We knew the cost of everything. Even if those other outfits had no overhead and were buying in container lots, there was still no way they could be making any money. I asked everyone, including my contact at Amazon, how this could be, but no one could give me a definitive answer.

We had overhead, and plenty of it. In addition to the rent, which didn't look like such a good deal anymore, there was electricity, gas, water, insurance and a lot of other nickel and dime things that don't seem like much by themselves but add up to a lot. It cost a lot of money to open the door on the first of each month and it was getting more difficult to make it back over the ensuing thirty days.

The polar vortex of 2014 didn't help either. There was snow on the ground from December to March with more piling up each day. Customers don't come out when it snows unless they absolutely have to. Why should they risk their lives when they could sit at their computers and have UPS or FedEx risk their lives instead? They could have whatever they wanted shipped right to their door for free. And they didn't have to pay sales tax.

We had become a dinosaur. Friendly, face-to-face customer service had gone the way of gas station attendants and rotary phones.

During the polar vortex our unemployment ran out. Some people stay on it for years. All the State of Illinois allowed us was six months. None of us had any income and the lousy weather killed any hope of being paid from the store. It was time for a new plan.

I had been to a financial planner the previous November to see which of the 567 plans Social Security offered to married people would work for us. He entered all our data into his computer and our best plan was to take it at age sixty-nine years, nine months. Age sixty-nine was too far away. Even nine months was longer than we could wait. Judy and I had to take it right away and forget the long-range plan.

Our son Jim didn't have that option. He needed an income. It's a good thing for him that my Dad's luck skipped me and went right to him. He found a job with an environmental company almost immediately. He likes it, the owners love him, and he has a good job with a future. We couldn't be happier for him.

That created another problem for Judy and me—no more days off. Each of us had been working four days a week. Now Judy and I would be working six days every week with only Sunday off. What a lot of people don't seem to understand is that small business owners have a life other than their stores. We have families and homes that require attention. Spending all that time in the store, and thinking about it when we're not there, leaves us little time to give family and home the attention they deserve. Sitting there one day, waiting for customers, we got talking and realized that what we were doing was stupid. We were making money for the landlord, all the utilities, our suppliers, and everyone else who had their hands out, but we got nothing for ourselves. Social Security was paying us whether we came to work or stayed home. We decided to stay home. And stop making plans.

Bankruptcy had always been an option. We were still making every effort to pay off the debt from the Worth store with the meager income from the new store but we could never get ahead. I won't go through the long, cumbersome bankruptcy process and hope that you never have to. On July 24, 2014, our debts were released and we were free. A bonus to bankruptcy unknown to us released us from our contract with the landlords. We were free to leave whenever we were ready. We were ready right then, but there was a sixty day period during which we couldn't say or do anything. It seemed to go on forever. Finally, on the sixty-first day, September 22, we made the announcement: Riley's Trick Shop was closing forever.

The Word Gets Out

The first thing I did that morning was post the following to Facebook:

This is it! After 77 years, Riley's Trick Shop will be closing its doors for the final time. We haven't set a date yet. That will be determined by how long it takes to sell down our inventory at greatly reduced prices...up to 90 percent off.

Since all our children have good jobs and no interest in taking over, Judy and I have decided to move on. We'd like to see what it's like to have a weekend together and maybe take a trip or two. It's been a long time.

Thanks to everyone for 77 great years. We hope to see you all at least one more time before we head off into our new adventure.

The reaction was swift and spread like wildfire. That one post got 530 likes and 389 shares. Altogether it reached 36,592 people over the next three days. I wish I could have had that reaction when I was actually trying to sell something.

That post garnered 194 comments, too. Here are some of my favorites:

<u>Nick Mendelke</u>: This makes me sad. I remember buying fake snot, dog poop, fake rats, etc. as a kid. I used to scare my grandmother on a regular basis. I remember a time when I used a fake mouse to make my grandmother jump out of our rocking chair. Now I am 35 and she is 91 and living in a nursing home where she doesn't always remember which grandson I am. Thank you for all the fun as a child and the memories I now have as an adult. Some of them, like the ones of my using your gags on my poor grandmother put a smile on my face today.

<u>Fred Rosenbaum</u>: So sad to hear you are closing. I got my first magic trick there in 1965 or so when you were located near Evergreen Park plaza. Since then I have become a life member of IBM (International Brotherhood of Magicians) and SAM (Society of American Magicians), served on the SAM board and various IBM committees. All because of a blue plastic box with colors and a hinged wooden board whose spots changed colors. I now live in NC or I would be sure to make a last trip.

I also remember taking my 5 year old daughter to your shop and buying her a magic wand. She got back home and waved it over 3 or 4 things saying "Abracadabra" then looked at me with the saddest eyes ever and said "Daddy, it's broke." She and her sister went on to perform at the SAM (Society of American Magicians) Young Professionals show in Las Vegas and won the TAOM (Texas Association of Magicians) Junior Stage contest.

Enjoy retirement knowing you brought joy to many of our lives.

<u>Kathy Sullivan</u>: I was in the hospital with the old man during the 1979 snowstorm. No visitors. No workers could make it to

work. I was confined to bed with a broken hip. Old Man Riley came to my room with a fake booger hanging out of his nose. I nearly peed in the bed. He also set it up so I could watch from my bed as he put a dollar bill on a fishing line and laid the dollar bill at the elevator door. I think he did that for 3 hours! We had so much fun! I would stop in and visit him occasionally at the store when I would stop in at The Little Inn. I am sure there are thousands of people that have fond memories of the shop but I also felt I had the best! Best wishes with the new chapter in your life!

Keith Celia: I used to go into Riley's at least once a week and spend my entire allowance each time. Your father would show me magic tricks all the time and I remember Jim would show me these great pranks...I owned them all and remember all of them fondly. Bringing my two girls into Riley's (both the Worth store and the Palos Hills one) is definitely a highlight. My girls love when I do various magic tricks for them. My love of magic comes directly from Jim and his father

I still fondly remember that mongoose in a box (got me every single time) gag that was on the counter for a long time and told myself I would buy it someday....Sigh.

Thanks to Nick, Fred, Kathy, and Keith for their memories and for helping me fill up a little space that I didn't have to write, revise, or edit. OK, I made some revisions. I can't help myself.

The other Facebook comments came from customers who wrote about more childhood memories or how they used to come to us when they were younger. There's the problem. "I used to shop there" doesn't do anything toward paying the rent today. Don't get me wrong, it's gratifying beyond measure to know that we touched so many lives and caused so many smiles and laughs. It's good to know, too, that so many young people got their first job from us and have found success in their adult lives. But that's all in the past. The time had come to move on.

Some of those reached by that Facebook post were in the media. That turned into an interview with the Chicago Tribune, a front-page story in the Southtown Star, an interview with WBBM radio that played over and over all day, and what could be my final appearance on the Skinny and Houli Show.

Did all this attention cause an uptick in business? Yes and no. A lot of things disappeared quickly but, at half price, it didn't do much for the bottom line. Magicians were the first to swoop in. Most of our magic items disappeared within the first two days. What didn't go then would most likely never go. Tricks and jokes went next. We had to order more just to have some for Halloween.

A lot of people came in to stock up on T-shirts and headlines but mostly they were coming in to see if it really was true. They asked the same questions over and over, some tearfully. "Why are you closing?" "Are you moving?" "What am I going to do without you?" That last question led me to ask them when was the last time they were there. The response was usually "a coupla years" but it had most likely been a lot longer than that. I told them they'd do just fine without us.

After hearing these questions over and over, I just wanted to scream, "Get over it already!" Judy was over it. I was over it and Riley's had been a huge part of my entire life. No one else could say that. We made a business decision and the time had come to move on.

I think the whole reason for our closing can be summed up by one man who came in shortly after the Facebook announcement. He answered his own question before asking it, but asked it anyway. "I haven't been in this store in forty years. So why are you closing?"

Our Final Halloween

In years past, the month of October was always busy. We worked from early to late Monday through Friday and all day Saturday. We went non-stop with hardly a break. In more recent years it had slowed down a lot but, with everything in the store half price, we thought this might be the year we'd see some of the traffic of those earlier years. Deep down inside we didn't want it to get that busy because it was just the two of us and not the ten employees we used to have. We'd never be able to keep up with it.

There was no fear of that. We were busier but it was nothing we couldn't handle. We got rid of a lot of costumes, masks, wigs, hats, and accessories that had been sitting around for years. Some people bought bags full of the heads we'd used to display our wigs and masks. Others took masks that were so old they were starting to fall apart. Even Jar Jar Binks masks sold. They'd been languishing on our shelves for fourteen years. Decorations that customers thought were part of our décor went as fast as we could put them back up on the wall.

What we had the most of was packaged costumes. We didn't buy any new ones the previous year so it was the same inventory we'd had in Worth. That included leftovers from Colleen's store in Frankfort, and she'd closed four years earlier. Some packages had never been opened, others had been tried on and repackaged, badly, more times than we could count. A lot of the packages were held together with price stickers from all the markdowns over the years. A costume that originally was priced at $39.95 could be had for under $10.00. They went out the door even though some had parts missing. I guess you can sell anything at half price or less.

Early in the month I started putting our printing equipment on Craig's List at greatly discounted prices. We had made our money with it and we just wanted it gone. It didn't take long. The T-shirt printer went first and the button machines shortly after. Our coffee mug printer sold quickly, too. Each machine was sold with the stipulation that they wouldn't be picked up until November.

That was a good thing because we ran shirt orders every day even though they were still full price. There were no discounts on custom work. No one complained and I was very busy every day with shirts for reunions, teams, and birthdays, lots of birthdays. Some people were buying birthday shirts a year or more in advance.

Our regular customers were stocking up on headlines, too, and for the first time ever we ran out of headline blanks. We considered ordering more but the minimum order was five hundred and we knew we'd never get rid of that many. When they finally ran out, I reconfigured the program to print headlines on plain 11x17 paper instead of the 11x15 blanks. We had a scanned copy of the headline blank that we used when sending proofs to customers. I just enlarged it to fill the 11x17 space and laid the customer's copy in the blank space as usual.

We didn't sell many of them because it was getting very near the end and the headline printer was on its way out. It was leaving vertical lines in solid black copy and no amount of cleaning would eliminate them. We considered ordering a new printer but we'd never make that money back in the short time we had left. Headlines had to be printed in red, blue, green, or whatever color or colors the customer wanted. We couldn't print photographs at all. Good thing I didn't order those five hundred blanks.

Our final Halloween wasn't great but we did better than expected even with everything at half price. We got rid of a lot of inventory and the place was starting to look empty. On a Saturday afternoon near closing I was alone and started to get nostalgic for the old days. Just then two things happened that made me realize it was time to go.

A man, about college age or a little older, came in and started looking around.

"Everything's half off?" he asked.

"At least half," I replied, "just take half off the lowest price marked."

He held up an item and asked, "It says this is ten dollars, what's half off that?"

Really? You can't figure out half of ten? I thought making thing half off would make it easy.

While he was trying to remember basic math, somebody's trophy wife came in with her three perfect children to look at costumes. Two were old enough to know how to act in a store, the other was barely walking. All three of those kids started trying on everything, leaving a wake of merchandise and empty packaging all over the floor. The mother was oblivious, like they were strangers who just happened to walk in the door the same time she did. She never said one thing to them. I asked them nicely to pick up after themselves and they acted as if I wasn't there or was just one of the servants. Then I did something I'd never done before at the store. It went against all my instincts as a retailer but I yelled at those kids like they were my own pillaging someone else's store. Apparently, they'd never been spoken to that way. They quickly picked up as best they could and huddled close to their mother. She was still oblivious. They eventually made their decisions, got what they wanted, and headed home in their perfect car, back to their perfect lives.

Now, we'd dealt with these situations before but it seemed to happening more and more. It was then that I knew we had made the right decision. It was time to call it a career.

Breaking It All Down

After Halloween there was still a lot of merchandise left over. It was mostly costumes, but there was a good cross-section of makeup, accessories, and other things. We decided to have another sale that would run from November 4th through the 14th. This time everything would be ninety percent off. Judy argued for seventy-five percent off, but I counter-argued that her discount would be more difficult to calculate at checkout. It was so easy at half off that we could do the math close enough in our heads, rounding up or down as necessary. This would be just as easy. At ninety percent off all we had to do was drop the last digit to determine a price. If something was $39.95, we'd just drop the 5 to make the final price $3.99, or four bucks rounded off. I told her all our customers would understand it and everything would move out much more quickly.

That theory went to pieces with the first customer who asked the discounted price for every item he looked at. "Drop the last digit," we said over and over. He came in three times the first day and every day after until the sale was over, each time unable to calculate the final price. Other customers didn't get the concept of ninety percent off either, but most did and things started going out the door by the industrial-sized garbage bagful as the word spread.

On Tuesday November 4, Stars and Stripes Silkscreening in Bridgeview came for the button equipment. They had a big truck and a couple of big guys who got everything out and on its way in minutes. That worked out well because someone was there at the same time to pick up one of our show cases. He had come alone I had to help him load it in his pickup truck.

There were slow times during this final sale and that's when we started breaking down the store for good. On Saturday the 8th I went outside during a lull to take down the die-cut lettering on the windows but had to come in several times because it got really busy. This would be our final Saturday in business.

It was the day that Riley's in Palos Hills died as I took down the "nonsense" plaque for the final time. Earlier in the week I'd received an email from someone who wanted to know if it was for sale. I wrote back and told him in no uncertain terms that it was a treasured piece of Riley's history and I wouldn't part with it at any price. He came back with an offer I couldn't refuse. I left it up until he came for it. After he put the plaque in his truck and drove away, my son called me a traitor and a whore, in jest I think, but as soon as I'd heard that offer I could hear the Old Man saying, "What the hell are *you* gonna do with it? Let it collect dust? Take the money and get it the hell outta there, ya mope!" I knew what I had to do. There was no changing my mind.

209

The buyer asked that his name and the selling price remain a secret. I can say that he's a magician and the plaque will reside in a place of honor. Ironically, the stack of hundreds he handed me came in a wrapper from the POS bank.

We were still open for business the following week but that's when we really began moving out. First up was taking down the gridwall racks. All eight had been spoken for but they needed to be broken apart so the buyer could get them in her van. Some went easy, others put up a fight. Their bolts had been stripped. It took all day but I got most of them apart. I would have finished but a group came in late and went a long way toward clearing us out.

Marty Kelly and another man brought in their kids who ran through the store grabbing stuff and piling it up on the counter. I went home an hour late but the store was much emptier than when they'd come in. Those kids went home as happy as could be. Marty also took some of the small drawers that were behind the counters. He left us with some nice parting gifts, too. Judy got a locket with a real four-leaf clover and I got a plaque with a mint Mercury dime from 1937, the year we opened.

It must be people named Marty because long-time customer Marty McCaw had stopped by earlier with a twelve of Heineken for me and a box of Fannie May for Judy. The beer and the candy are gone but we'll treasure the locket and the plaque for a long time.

The next day, Wednesday, I got the last of the gridwall taken apart, just in time for the buyer to pick them up. She was also interested in the metal shelving behind the counter and asked what I wanted for it. I told her she could have it if she took it apart herself and hauled it out. She came back the following Monday, got it all down, packed it in her van, and took whatever of those small drawers would fit in the remaining space. It took her three hours, time that I was able to devote to something else.

That same day we said goodbye to our old headline press. I'd sold it to T & T Press Restoration of Hugo, Minnesota, northeast of Minneapolis. They had sent a large packing crate the day before. All I had to do was get the press into it and close it back up. Easier said than done. That old Vandercook was built to last and weighed a ton. There was no way I could lift it. Fortunately, my son had put it on a mover's dolly when we sold the case it was displayed in. I laid the crate on its side and rolled the dolly up to it. I had already removed the top. Using the press's weight as leverage, I was able to lift the dolly from the side away from the crate and lay the press up against the 2x6's inside. Using leverage again, I raised the crate to its upright position and secured the press to the 2x6's. So what if it was upside down. I had put it this two hundred-plus pound machine into the crate by myself. Who needs muscle when you have a brain? After fabricating parts to return it to its original glory, T & T sent the old Vandercook to its new home at an international advertising company in Boulder, Colorado.

Also sold that day were our glass and wood show cases. A man came in to pay in full and say he'd be back when he could get a truck and some help. He didn't quibble about the price either. They were a bargain and he knew it.

Friday was our last day open to the public. Our final customer spent $43.00. That was still at 90% off so he walked out with a lot of stuff.

Then the real work began and so did the real pain. Judy and I had cleaned out the drawers in the stockroom and it was time to break them down. Anybody who's ever shopped at our stores beginning on 79th and Aberdeen has seen them. They were green, 25 inches deep by 16 inches wide and 11 inches high, and had cardboard or metal fronts. They were called Pronto Files and Stax on Steel but they all had one thing in common. Rods ran through the sides and attached to the fronts and backs. The drawers arrived flat and those rods were what held them together. They were less than an eighth of an inch thick and, once the drawers were assembled, they were not meant to come out, easily or otherwise.

I had tried giving them away on Craig's List but had no takers. I guess nobody needs ready-made assembled drawers these days. They had to be taken apart and flattened or it was going to be difficult and expensive to get rid of them. I had to cut each rod with a bolt cutter. Sure, cutting a thin metal rod doesn't sound all that difficult, and it isn't, but we had at least 150 drawers in the stockroom and under the T-shirt counter. Over the next week I made cuts in each corner of every drawer. That's at least six hundred cuts and my shoulders were seriously hurting. Toward the end, those rods felt like kryptonite to Superman. Each drawer had a cardboard sleeve that had to be flattened, too. And the metal fronts of some of the drawers had to be cut off for recycling. I didn't feel anything like Superman after that.

After I removed the drawers from under the T-shirt counter I had to start breaking down the counter itself. First, I removed the carpeting that we'd used as trim on the front. It was held on with staples. Easy. Next was the plywood on the front and top. It was bolted on and covered with self-adhesive floor tile. Harder. Finally, there was the angle-iron skeleton that I had disassembled at the Worth store and painstakingly fashioned into new counters in Palos Hills. Gigantic pain in the ass. This stuff is expensive to buy new and I tried to get rid of it cheap at first, free as a last resort. Again, there were no takers. It would just be piled up for recycling. This job didn't hurt my shoulders as much as cutting the drawers did, but all the bending and stretching played havoc with my knees and back.

The day I was doing that, Judy said she wanted me to make some Riley's shirts for the people who were coming to our house for Thanksgiving. Judy's sister, Geri Hlavac, normally has Thanksgiving but she had conveniently broken her wrist earlier in the month and asked us to take it, as if we didn't have enough to do this particular November. I didn't want to take time out to do shirts but Judy insisted. There were only twenty-seven people coming and it wouldn't take that long she said. When it began to take that long and longer, I took a count and found that she had piled sixty-two T-shirts and sweatshirts for me to print. We were still giving them away to the Riley cousins at Christmas.

Those were the last T-shirts I ever printed. Angela from Tomber Promotions in Oak Lawn came to pick up the machine later that afternoon. She brought a pickup truck and three big guys who manhandled that very heavy machine and its very heavy base out the back door and on to its new home.

We spent the rest of the week cleaning, removing, disposing, and recycling.

In the middle of all this there was still merchandise to get rid of. We took a bunch of it home or gave it to our kids but there was still more. It must have been breeding overnight.

During Halloween one of our customers asked what we would do with anything we didn't sell. We told him we'd find somebody to donate it to. He recommended the Garden Center and gave us their number. He told us that he was one of their clients and they would love to take it off our hands because they throw a lot of parties.

According to their website, "Garden Center Services was established in 1956 as a grassroots effort to support children with developmental disabilities and their families. What started as an organization run entirely from a space above the garage at Reavis High School has blossomed into a multi-program agency that has a reputation for providing outstanding services to adults with disabilities." We couldn't think of a better home for our leftovers.

I called and spoke to Ralph Storino, one of their directors, who came out to see what we had. He said, "We'll take it all," and filled his car with costumes. A couple of days later a crew of their clients came out for the rest of it in a fifteen passenger van. Ralph brought Jennifer Georgis, Director of Development, in another vehicle.

What a blast it was watching those young men and women rummage through the piles of masks, hats, wigs, costumes, and more. Even though life had dealt them a bad hand, they worked together with such joy and enthusiasm that Judy and I knew we'd done the right thing. They were efficient, too. They swept in and out in less than half an hour. They filled the empty seats in the van and carried the rest on their laps. Jennifer helped Ralph fill his car, too.

They couldn't thank us enough and there were hugs and handshakes all around. They said they would be using these things for years to come. In reality, we thank them. Not only did they help us immensely, they brought a joyous, bright moment into a week of drudgery. We resumed our labors with smiles on our faces and happy tears in our eyes.

The last of our equipment to go to a new home were my dad's custom-made show cases that had been with us since Western Avenue. They went to a shop in Indiana that sells electronic cigarettes. The man who had paid for them earlier brought a partner and a big truck. I'd hoped they'd take some of those small drawers, too. No dice. Judy and I spent the next two hours getting them ready for recycling.

Since the 1950s those drawers had sat behind our counters holding whoopee cushions, joy buzzers, fake snot, makeup, magic, and anything else that would fit. For full disclosure, they were officially "card index transfer cases for 6x9-inch cards, manufactured by the Globe-Wernicke Company of Cincinnati, Ohio." That was according to the lettering on the back flap of each drawer. I had been in and out of those drawers for more than fifty years and knew the text was there, but never paid any attention until that day. It was good to know their original purpose now that they were about to be reduced to flat pieces of cardboard junk.

Like the larger drawers these, too, were built to last. There were no rods holding them together, just cardboard, some kind of tape, and the wood-grained contact paper Jim Wallace had covered them with in the 70s. Some were green, some were blue. As Judy and I took our box cutters to each corner, we found that the green ones put up more of a fight. They must have been older and made better. We swore at all the boxes that gave us trouble, more so at the green ones.

When we were finished with the drawers, we had to break down the sleeves they came in. The sophisticated method we chose was stomping on them. Some went easily, others not so much. Damn those green ones!

That was the last of the big items. What was left was the most dreaded part of any moving job: the small stuff. It was the little things that businesses use every day, things that go unnoticed until they're missing or have to be moved. Some things will be sold, recycled, or trashed while others will be used at home.

Jim came by Saturday morning and picked up all the metal, the other recyclables, and anything else he wanted for himself. Then he headed out for the last time. Judy's last day had been the day before. She needed to stay home and prepare the Thanksgiving feast. The next few days were left to me as I brought carload after carload home and schlepped it to the basement, the spare bedroom, or the garage.

In spite of the carpeting and acoustical ceiling tiles, there was a hint of an echo as the place was emptying out. Riley's Trick Shop was truly coming to an end.

It wasn't long after we closed that we made it onto a website called "Lost Chicago" which shows pictures of former city and suburban stores, restaurants, and attractions. I thought we'd be in the shopping section, but they put us under entertainment. We joined the ranks of Kiddie Land, Riverview, Old Chicago, and many others long gone but not forgotten.

May The Road Rise Up To Meet You...

The final day had arrived. I had told the management that we'd be out by Thanksgiving. Tuesday November 25, 2014, was the target date, with the following day as a cushion, just in case we couldn't get everything out in time.

The first order of business was meeting with the guys from 1-800-GOT-JUNK. All those drawers large and small along with everything else we couldn't get rid of had been stacked in one of the stockrooms. Getting rid of all that by myself would have taken weeks. They did it under an hour. It cost $508 but I thought it was well worth it.

I made a couple more trips home with the small stuff and came back for one final load. Once that was in the car, it was just me and that chair that was there the day I was given the key. I was waiting for Ice Mountain to come for the water cooler. There was no telling when they'd show up so I brought a book to read while I waited, but my mind kept drifting from the pages.

I thought about my parents in their first empty storefront at 79th and Rhodes. Were they afraid? Were they hopeful? Anxious? Did they have any idea their dream would last as long as it did? I wondered how they would feel if they knew how it ended.

Faces of past employees drifted through my mind, hundreds of them. Some of them stayed with us for hours or days, others many years. I keep in contact with a few of them. The rest seem to have vanished. I like to think they remember their time with us fondly-- the jokes, the laughter, the cama-raderie of working our tails off during Halloween, and the soul-searching discussions during slow times. Most we knew only at work and others became like family, inviting us to their weddings and into their homes, attending our wakes and we attending theirs.

Speaking of family, I had my grandson, Ethan, work a couple of Saturdays in October just to say we'd employed five generations of family over the last seventy-seven years.

Then there were the customers, too numerous to count. Most I recalled fondly, others not so much. As with the employees, there were those who came in as customers but became friends. The counter between us melted away. And there were others who made us cringe just by pulling into the parking lot. Such are the joys of retail. It doesn't matter if you're happy to see them come or overjoyed to see them leave, you still have to treat each and every one as a customer. We tried our best to do that.

We got to know everyone in Ned Kubicki's family through the headlines he had us make, the same for the Pelegrino family through their T-shirt or-ders. We watched whole families grow up as we made photo shirts of their children for their parents and grandparents over the years.

We made tens of thousands of wedding headlines for area photogra-phers. Most were done via phone, mail, fax, and email. We met some of those photographers briefly and others never at all, but Don Pointer and his wife, Nora, who shot Colleen's and Jim's weddings became very dear friends.

There were the regular customers, there were the irregulars, and then there were the characters. Paul Bachman used to entertain us with his feats of juggling. He once brought in, and rode, a bicycle that was a mere six-inches high. Roger Siegal, magician, balloon artist, and comedian, used to try out his new jokes on us. There was Bob and his long-winded stories that took the scenic route to the punchline. Even his knock-knock jokes lasted a full five minutes. Toward the end there was Jerry whose hatred for the President was boundless. He kept me busy for hours printing his latest anti-Obama invective on shirts for all the world to see—even in church. Even closer to the end, there was Lois Lang. She was so upset about our closing that she stopped by every day to get T-shirts and buy another display rack. When I asked her what she was going to do with them, she'd reply, "Damned if I know." There were so many more that I could fill another book, if I could remember them all. It would be a sterile, boring world without the characters.

So many other thoughts filtered through my mind: the old locations, the neighborhoods, the fun, the laughter, the good times, and the bad. But foremost were the people, gone but not forgotten, the employees, the customers, the suppliers, and all who took part in our journey. Without them…who knows? God bless them all.

My thoughts drifted to the future, too. They didn't want to stay in the present; it was just too painful. The hurt wasn't emotional, it was physical. I'd overworked muscles and joints that hadn't been used in a while and they all let me know how unhappy they were. It took two days of soaking in a hot tub on our family's Christmas vacation to get them to "quityerbellyachin," as Dad used to say.

The near future was crystal clear. Everything that I'd brought home and piled in the rec room, kitchen, and living room had to be brought into the basement. Thanksgiving was only two days away and we needed the space for our guests. There's no rest for weary muscles.

The long-term future was murkier. Customers asked if I was going to be bored once the store was closed. No way. I have enough hobbies and "outside activities" to keep me occupied for a long time. I refuse to spend my free time sitting in front of the TV…unless the Blackhawks are on. There are a lot of guest rooms around the country with open invitations, too. I've been to all fifty states but still haven't seen all there is to see in this great country of ours. Judy still has states to cross off her list. Travel and reconnecting with friends will be top priorities.

Once the dust settles farther down the road, then what? Will we be able to survive on Social Security? Will he have to get jobs? Who would hire us anyway? Will this book sell enough copies to let us live the high life on the royalties? We all know the answer to that one.

The reality is that a very large door has just closed behind us, it's locked from the inside, and we don't have a key. Ahead of us is a long, long hallway with lots of open doors. We intend to find out what's behind each and every one of them.

My reverie was interrupted by the diesel motor of the Ice Mountain truck. It was time to go. As the driver was rolling out the water cooler, I told him, "You're it. Once you're done, I have nothing left to do but lock up and get the hell out of here."

Wait. Did I really say that? No, I didn't. It came through me but it wasn't from me. I'd been expecting some kind of inspirational message from my Dad, something to carry me through the years to come. "Get the hell out of here" was all I was going to get. I locked the door for the final time and, with Bob Seger's "Roll Me Away" blasting from the car stereo, I turned toward the sunset on 111th Street and got the hell out of there.

The End

"It felt so good to be finally feelin' free."

Bob Seger

Thank you for reading my book. At this point, the publisher expected me to put in an "About the Author" page. If you've read this far, you should know everything there is to know.

As I mentioned at the start, you can see more of the story in pictures by going to our photo album in the Riley's Trick Shop page on Facebook. I'm always finding new things to add so be sure to check back often.